Adin Xeris

Battling for LGBTQ Freedom in Tarvel – Unauthorized

Ayesha Gupta

ISBN: 9781779697820
Imprint: Telephasic Workshop
Copyright © 2024 Ayesha Gupta.
All Rights Reserved.

Contents

Section 1: A Closeted Hometown

Introduction: The Setting of Tarvel

In the quaint town of Tarvel, where the air is thick with the scent of conservative values and unspoken truths, our hero, Adin Xeris, found himself nestled in the cocoon of a closeted existence. Picture this: a picturesque town where the most controversial topic is whether to put pineapple on pizza. Here, the LGBTQ community is less of a vibrant tapestry and more like a hidden Easter egg—nobody wants to admit it exists, but they all secretly hope to find it.

Adin's Childhood in Tarvel

Adin grew up in a household that valued tradition over truth. His parents, staunch believers in the "nuclear family" model, had a vision for their son that didn't quite include rainbow flags or pride parades. Instead, it was all about Sunday school, football games, and the occasional bake sale. Adin's childhood was a series of internal conflicts, a tug-of-war between who he was and who he was expected to be.

Conservative Values and Social Pressure

In Tarvel, the social fabric was woven tightly with conservative threads. Any deviation from the norm was met with the kind of scrutiny usually reserved for reality TV stars caught in a scandal. Adin felt the weight of this pressure like a heavy backpack filled with bricks. He learned early on that being different was akin to being a unicorn in a field of horses—beautiful, but definitely not welcome.

Adin Questions His Sexual Orientation

As Adin entered his teenage years, the questions began to swirl like a tornado in his mind. "Am I gay? Am I straight? Do I even like the color pink?" The confusion was palpable, and in a town where the word "gay" was often followed by a smirk or a joke, he found himself questioning everything. It was like trying to solve a Rubik's cube blindfolded—frustrating and confusing, with no one to help.

The Fear of Being Different

The fear of being different loomed over Adin like a dark cloud. He watched as classmates navigated their identities with ease, while he felt like a fish out of water, gasping for air in a world that demanded conformity. The thought of coming out was terrifying—imagine standing in front of a firing squad and saying, "Hey, I'm not who you think I am!" The stakes felt high, and the potential fallout was enough to keep him locked away in the closet, where the only thing that thrived was his anxiety.

A Friend's Acceptance Changes Everything

Everything changed one fateful day when Adin confided in his childhood friend, Mia. With the kind of acceptance that could only be found in the pages of a cheesy coming-of-age movie, Mia responded, "So what? You're still my best friend, and

I love you no matter what." It was a simple statement, but it felt like the first ray of sunshine breaking through a stormy sky. For the first time, Adin realized that acceptance was possible, and it sparked a flicker of hope in his heart.

Discovering the LGBTQ Community

With Mia by his side, Adin began to explore the LGBTQ community, a world that was vibrant and alive, filled with colors he didn't know existed. It was like stepping into a new dimension where love was celebrated, not shamed. He attended underground gatherings, where the music was loud, the laughter was contagious, and the sense of belonging was intoxicating. Here, he discovered that he wasn't alone; there were others like him, navigating the same treacherous waters.

Adin's Decision to Fight for Equality

Empowered by this newfound community, Adin made a pivotal decision: he would fight for LGBTQ rights in Tarvel. He envisioned a world where kids wouldn't have to hide who they were, where love was love, and acceptance was the norm. It was a daunting task, but with every rallying cry, Adin felt the fire of activism ignite within him.

The Birth of Adin Xeris, the Activist

And thus, Adin Xeris was born—not just as a name, but as a symbol of resistance against the oppressive norms of Tarvel. He began to speak out, to challenge the status quo, and to rally others to join him in the fight for equality. The shy boy who once hid in the shadows was now stepping into the light, ready to take on the world, one protest at a time.

The Impact of Adin's Supportive Family

Even amidst the chaos, Adin found solace in the support of his family. While they struggled to understand his journey, their love provided a safety net that allowed him to soar. It was a reminder that even in a world filled with judgment, love could still shine through. Adin learned that acceptance often starts at home, and with that knowledge, he was ready to take on the world, armed with the strength of his family and the love of his community.

Conclusion: The Journey Ahead

As Adin stood on the precipice of activism, he knew that the road ahead would be fraught with challenges. But he was no longer just a boy from a closeted hometown; he was Adin Xeris, a beacon of hope for those who felt unheard and unseen. The battle for LGBTQ rights in Tarvel was just beginning, and with every step, he was ready to make history.

Reflection on a Closeted Hometown

In a town like Tarvel, where the closets were packed tighter than a can of sardines, Adin's journey was a testament to the power of authenticity. It was a reminder that even in the most conservative settings, the fight for love and acceptance could flourish, one courageous heart at a time.

End of Section

Section 1: A Closeted Hometown

In the quaint, conservative town of Tarvel, the air was thick with unspoken norms and expectations. The very essence of growing up in a place like Tarvel could be likened to living in a bubble—one that was not only restrictive but also suffocating. Here, the idea of being different was not just frowned upon; it was akin to treason. In this environment, Adin Xeris would navigate the tumultuous waters of adolescence, grappling with his identity while surrounded by a community that thrived on conformity.

1.1.1 Adin's Childhood in Tarvel

Adin's childhood was marked by the innocence of youth, yet it was overshadowed by the weight of societal expectations. Tarvel was a town where the notion of "normal" was defined by a rigid set of standards. Families were often nuclear, with the archetypal mother and father dynamic reigning supreme. Adin, a sensitive child with a flair for the dramatic, felt the pressure to fit into this mold. He was the kid who preferred to dance to his own rhythm, but in Tarvel, dancing to a different beat could earn you a one-way ticket to social exile.

1.1.2 Conservative Values and Social Pressure

The conservative values that permeated Tarvel were not just a backdrop; they were the very fabric of life. The local church was the cornerstone of the community, and its teachings echoed through the streets, instilling a fear of difference in the hearts of many. The pressure to conform was palpable, and for Adin, it manifested as a constant internal struggle. He often found himself questioning the very essence of who he was, wondering if the feelings he harbored were merely a phase or something more profound.

1.1.3 Adin Questions His Sexual Orientation

As Adin transitioned into his teenage years, the questions surrounding his sexual orientation became more pronounced. In a town where heterosexuality was the default, the mere act of questioning one's identity felt like a rebellion. Adin would often find himself in a whirlwind of confusion, grappling with the fear of being different while simultaneously yearning for authenticity. This dichotomy created a mental tug-of-war, where each side pulled him in opposite directions.

1.1.4 The Fear of Being Different

The fear of being different in Tarvel was not just a personal battle; it was a communal one. Adin witnessed friends and peers suppressing their true selves to avoid ridicule. The fear of ostracization loomed large, creating a culture of silence. Adin often felt like a ghost, haunting the hallways of his own life, yearning to be seen yet terrified of what being seen would mean. It was a paradox that many LGBTQ+ individuals know all too well: the desire for acceptance clashing with the fear of rejection.

1.1.5 A Friend's Acceptance Changes Everything

However, everything began to shift when Adin encountered a friend who saw him for who he truly was. This friend, a fellow outcast in their own right, became a beacon of hope. Their acceptance was a revelation, illuminating the path toward self-acceptance for Adin. It was in this friendship that Adin found the courage to explore his identity, realizing that he was not alone in his struggles. This pivotal moment marked the beginning of his journey toward embracing his true self.

1.1.6 Discovering the LGBTQ Community

As Adin delved deeper into his identity, he stumbled upon the existence of the LGBTQ community, albeit in hushed whispers and secretive gatherings. The discovery was both exhilarating and terrifying. It was a world where people celebrated their differences rather than hide them. Adin began to attend clandestine meetings, where he found solace in the stories of others who had traversed similar paths. The LGBTQ community became a sanctuary, a place where he could shed the weight of societal expectations and embrace his authentic self.

1.1.7 Adin's Decision to Fight for Equality

With newfound strength, Adin made a decision that would alter the course of his life: he would fight for equality. The realization that he could advocate for change ignited a fire within him. Adin understood that his struggles were not isolated; they were part of a larger narrative that needed to be told. He began to envision a future where individuals could live openly and authentically, free from the shackles of societal judgment.

1.1.8 The Birth of Adin Xeris, the Activist

Thus, Adin Xeris was born—not just as an individual, but as a symbol of hope and resistance. The transformation from a closeted boy to a passionate activist was not instantaneous; it was a journey fraught with challenges and triumphs. Adin began to channel his experiences into activism, using his voice to uplift others who felt silenced. He became a catalyst for change, determined to dismantle the oppressive structures that had long governed Tarvel.

1.1.9 The Impact of Adin's Supportive Family

Crucially, Adin's journey was also shaped by the impact of his supportive family. Unlike many in Tarvel, Adin was fortunate to have parents who embraced him for who he was. Their unwavering support provided a safety net, allowing him to explore his identity without the fear of losing their love. This familial acceptance became a cornerstone of his activism, fueling his desire to create a world where every individual could experience the same level of support and acceptance.

In conclusion, the story of Adin Xeris in his closeted hometown of Tarvel is a testament to the resilience of the human spirit. It highlights the struggles of navigating identity in a conservative environment while illustrating the transformative power of acceptance and community. As Adin's journey unfolds, it becomes clear that the fight for LGBTQ rights is not just a political battle; it is a deeply personal one, rooted in the desire for love, acceptance, and the freedom to be oneself.

ERROR. thisXsection() returned an empty string with textbook depth = 3.

ERROR. thisXsection() returned an empty string with textbook depth = 3.

ERROR. thisXsection() returned an empty string with textbook depth = 3.

Conservative Values and Social Pressure

In the quaint town of Tarvel, where the air is thick with the scent of freshly mowed lawns and the whispers of conservative values echo louder than the church bells, Adin Xeris found himself wrestling with the societal expectations that surrounded him. The fabric of Tarvel was woven with threads of traditionalism, where family values were celebrated, and anything outside the heteronormative spectrum was often met with disdain. This subsection delves into the conservative values that shaped Adin's upbringing and the social pressure that stifled his authentic self.

The Weight of Tradition

In many small towns like Tarvel, conservative values are not just beliefs; they are a way of life. Families pride themselves on their legacy, often passing down ideologies that reinforce a binary understanding of gender and sexuality. Adin grew up in a household that revered these traditions, where discussions about sexuality were often replaced with conversations about sports, church activities, and the importance of marrying "the right kind of person."

This environment created an implicit equation of worth and acceptance based on conformity:

$$\text{Acceptance} \propto \text{Conformity to Conservative Norms} \qquad (1)$$

For Adin, the pressure to conform meant that any deviation from the norm could lead to ostracization. The fear of being different loomed large, creating an internal conflict that made the journey to self-acceptance feel like a steep mountain to climb.

Social Pressure and Its Implications

The social pressure in Tarvel manifested in various ways. From subtle glances during church services to outright exclusion from community events, the message was clear: be like everyone else, or face the consequences. Adin often felt the weight of this pressure, as he navigated his teenage years filled with curiosity and confusion about his identity.

This pressure was compounded by the very institutions that were meant to support him. Schools, often seen as safe havens for self-exploration, became battlegrounds where conservative values were enforced through bullying and ridicule. Adin, like many LGBTQ youth, faced the harsh reality that his peers were not always allies. The social dynamics in Tarvel created an environment where being different was synonymous with being wrong.

The Role of Family

Family, the cornerstone of conservative values, played a pivotal role in shaping Adin's experience. His parents, well-intentioned but steeped in traditional beliefs, often emphasized the importance of fitting in. Phrases like "What will the neighbors think?" echoed in their home, reinforcing the notion that reputation and conformity were paramount.

This familial pressure can be illustrated by the following equation that captures the relationship between familial expectations and personal identity:

$$\text{Personal Identity} = f(\text{Familial Expectations, Social Norms}) \qquad (2)$$

For Adin, this function was fraught with complications. The more he tried to align his identity with his family's expectations, the more he felt like a stranger in his own skin. The conflict between wanting to please his family and the desire to embrace his true self became a source of profound inner turmoil.

Resistance and Rebellion

However, amidst the conservative backdrop of Tarvel, seeds of rebellion began to sprout. Adin's experiences with social pressure ignited a fire within him—a desire not only to accept himself but to challenge the very values that sought to suppress him. He began to seek out literature, art, and voices that resonated with his struggles, discovering a world beyond the confines of Tarvel's conservative walls.

This awakening can be represented by the following transformation:

$$\text{Awareness} = \text{Exploration} + \text{Connection} \qquad (3)$$

Through exploration, Adin connected with like-minded individuals who shared similar experiences, ultimately leading to a collective resistance against the conservative values that had once held him captive. This newfound community became a lifeline, providing the support and understanding that was often absent in his immediate environment.

Conclusion

In conclusion, the conservative values and social pressure that permeated Adin's upbringing in Tarvel were formidable forces that shaped his journey. The weight of tradition, the implications of social pressure, and the role of family created a complex landscape that he had to navigate. Yet, through resistance and rebellion, Adin began to carve out a space for himself, laying the groundwork for the activist he would become. The struggles he faced in reconciling these conservative values with his emerging identity were not just personal battles; they were reflective of a larger societal issue that many LGBTQ individuals confront in similar environments. As Adin's story unfolds, it becomes clear that the fight for authenticity is often intertwined with the fight against deeply rooted societal norms.

Adin Questions His Sexual Orientation

As Adin navigated the murky waters of adolescence in the conservative enclave of Tarvel, he found himself grappling with an internal conflict that many young people face but few articulate: the question of his sexual orientation. It was a labyrinth of emotions, societal expectations, and self-discovery, one that would shape not only his identity but also his future as an activist.

Theoretical Framework

To understand Adin's journey, we can draw upon several theories of sexual orientation development. One prominent model is the **Cass Sexual Identity Model**, which outlines six stages of sexual identity formation:

- Identity Confusion

- Identity Comparison

- Identity Tolerance

- Identity Acceptance

- Identity Pride

- Identity Synthesis

Adin found himself oscillating between the first two stages—identity confusion and identity comparison. He experienced a profound sense of confusion as he began to recognize feelings that deviated from the heteronormative expectations of his upbringing. This confusion was compounded by the pervasive conservative values that permeated his community, which dictated that anything outside of heterosexuality was not just unusual, but wrong.

The Role of Social Pressure

Social pressure played a significant role in Adin's questioning. In Tarvel, the idea of masculinity was tightly wound with heterosexual norms. Adin often felt the weight of this expectation pressing down on him, manifesting in the form of anxiety and fear. He remembered an incident in middle school when a classmate had teased him for not being interested in sports, a quintessential marker of masculinity in his community. The laughter of his peers echoed in his mind, reinforcing the notion that to be different was to invite ridicule.

Adin's internal struggle was not just a personal battle; it was a reflection of the larger societal context. According to **Erikson's Psychosocial Development Theory**, the stage of identity vs. role confusion is crucial during adolescence. Adin was at a crossroads, trying to reconcile his emerging identity with the roles prescribed by his family and community. This tension created a cognitive dissonance that left him feeling isolated.

Exploration and Self-Reflection

In the midst of this turmoil, Adin began to explore his feelings through self-reflection and connection with art. He discovered that writing poetry allowed him to express emotions that he struggled to verbalize. Lines like, "In a world of black and white, I paint in shades of gray," became a mantra for him. This artistic outlet provided a safe space for exploration, allowing him to question societal norms without the immediate fear of backlash.

Moreover, the advent of the internet opened new avenues for Adin. He stumbled upon online forums and communities where individuals shared their experiences of questioning their sexual orientation. For the first time, he encountered stories that mirrored his own, which provided a sense of validation. These narratives illustrated the spectrum of sexual orientation, challenging the binary view that had been ingrained in him.

The Impact of a Friend's Acceptance

A pivotal moment in Adin's journey came when he confided in a close friend, Jamie. Jamie, who had been openly questioning their own identity, responded with empathy and understanding. This acceptance was transformative for Adin. He realized that he was not alone in his struggles, and this revelation catalyzed a shift in his perspective.

Adin's experience aligns with the **Social Identity Theory**, which posits that individuals derive part of their identity from the social groups they belong to. Jamie's acceptance helped Adin to forge a new social identity—one that embraced his queerness rather than shying away from it. This acceptance was not just a personal triumph; it was a stepping stone toward his eventual activism.

Conclusion

As Adin wrestled with his sexual orientation, he began to understand that questioning was not a sign of weakness, but rather a fundamental part of the human experience. This period of introspection laid the groundwork for his future activism, as he recognized the importance of creating spaces where others could question and explore their identities without fear.

Through the lens of theory and personal experience, Adin's journey of questioning his sexual orientation was a complex interplay of societal pressures, self-discovery, and the power of acceptance. It was a critical chapter in his life that would ultimately propel him into the realm of activism, where he would fight for the rights of others who faced similar struggles.

The Fear of Being Different

The journey of self-discovery for many individuals, particularly those within the LGBTQ+ community, is often fraught with the profound fear of being different. This fear can be deeply rooted in societal norms, cultural expectations, and personal experiences. It is a multifaceted issue that not only impacts one's self-identity but also influences interactions with family, friends, and the broader community.

Theoretical Framework

From a psychological perspective, the fear of being different can be understood through the lens of *social identity theory*, which posits that individuals derive a sense of self from their group memberships. When an individual's identity diverges from the dominant culture, it can lead to feelings of alienation and anxiety. According to *Tajfel and Turner* (1979), this theory emphasizes the importance of belonging to a group that shares similar values and beliefs. For LGBTQ+ individuals, the fear of being different often stems from the risk of social exclusion or discrimination, leading to internalized homophobia and self-stigmatization.

Cultural and Societal Influences

In conservative environments, like Adin's hometown of Tarvel, traditional values often dictate acceptable behaviors and identities. The pressure to conform can be overwhelming, creating a psychological barrier that prevents individuals from fully embracing their authentic selves. This societal pressure manifests in various forms, including:

+ **Family Expectations:** Many LGBTQ+ individuals face the daunting task of reconciling their identities with the expectations of their families. The fear of disappointing loved ones can lead to a reluctance to come out, perpetuating a cycle of secrecy and shame.

+ **Peer Pressure:** Adolescents, in particular, are heavily influenced by their peers. The desire to fit in can lead to the suppression of one's true identity, fostering a sense of isolation and loneliness.

+ **Media Representation:** The lack of positive representation in media can exacerbate feelings of being different. When LGBTQ+ characters are depicted negatively or stereotypically, it reinforces the notion that being different is undesirable.

Personal Examples

Adin's experience in Tarvel exemplifies the struggle against the fear of being different. Growing up in a conservative household, Adin often felt the weight of expectations pressing down on him. He recalls moments in high school where he would overhear conversations mocking those who didn't conform to traditional gender roles. The pervasive attitude of his peers created an environment where expressing one's true self felt like an act of rebellion.

One pivotal moment for Adin occurred during a school assembly where a guest speaker discussed the importance of diversity and acceptance. The speaker's message resonated deeply with him, igniting a flicker of hope that perhaps being different could be celebrated rather than condemned. However, the fear of backlash from his classmates lingered, making it difficult for him to fully embrace this newfound perspective.

Consequences of Fear

The fear of being different can lead to several adverse outcomes, including:

+ **Mental Health Issues:** Studies have shown that individuals who experience significant internal conflict regarding their identities are more likely to suffer from anxiety, depression, and other mental health disorders (Meyer, 2003). The fear of rejection can lead to a pervasive sense of inadequacy and despair.

+ **Social Isolation:** The desire to hide one's true self often results in withdrawing from social interactions. This isolation can further exacerbate feelings of loneliness and despair, creating a vicious cycle that is hard to escape.

+ **Delayed Self-Acceptance:** The longer individuals suppress their identities, the more challenging it becomes to accept themselves. This delay can hinder personal growth and the ability to engage authentically with others.

Overcoming the Fear

Despite the challenges posed by the fear of being different, many individuals find ways to confront and overcome this fear. Supportive networks, such as LGBTQ+ organizations, play a crucial role in providing safe spaces for individuals to explore their identities without judgment. These communities foster resilience and empowerment, allowing members to share their experiences and support one another in the journey toward self-acceptance.

Adin's eventual involvement with the local LGBTQ+ community in Tarvel marked a significant turning point in his life. Through participation in underground gatherings and advocacy efforts, he discovered that he was not alone in his fears. The camaraderie he found within this community helped him to dismantle the internalized fears that had held him captive for so long.

In conclusion, the fear of being different is a significant barrier that many individuals face, particularly within the LGBTQ+ community. Understanding the psychological and social factors that contribute to this fear is essential for fostering acceptance and promoting mental well-being. By creating inclusive environments and supporting one another, individuals can learn to embrace their differences, transforming fear into a source of strength.

$$\text{Fear of Being Different} = f(\text{Societal Norms, Cultural Expectations, Personal Experiences}) \tag{4}$$

The equation above illustrates the interplay between various factors contributing to the fear of being different. Each component influences an individual's perception of self and their willingness to embrace their identity.

A Friend's Acceptance Changes Everything

In the small, conservative town of Tarvel, where the air was thick with judgment and the sidewalks echoed with whispers, Adin Xeris found himself at a crossroads. His childhood had been a tapestry of confusion, woven together with threads of fear and uncertainty about his identity. But as fate would have it, one pivotal encounter would change the trajectory of his life forever.

The Power of Acceptance

Acceptance is a powerful force. According to social psychologist William James, "The greatest discovery of my generation is that a human being can alter his life by altering his attitude." This notion is particularly relevant in the context of LGBTQ+

individuals, who often grapple with internalized homophobia and societal rejection. For Adin, the turning point came when he confided in his childhood friend, Maya.

Maya was the kind of friend who could make you laugh until you cried, and during one of their late-night talks filled with pizza and secrets, Adin took a deep breath and revealed his truth. "Maya, I think I might be... different." The words hung in the air like a fragile balloon, ready to pop at any moment.

To his surprise, Maya didn't flinch. Instead, she leaned in closer, her eyes sparkling with understanding. "Adin, you're still you. And I'm still here," she said, her voice steady and reassuring. This moment of acceptance shattered the walls Adin had built around himself. In that instant, he realized that being different didn't mean being alone.

The Ripple Effect of Acceptance

Maya's acceptance ignited a ripple effect in Adin's life. It served as a catalyst for self-acceptance, allowing him to embrace his identity without the crushing weight of shame. This aligns with the concept of *social support*, which is crucial for psychological well-being. Research indicates that supportive friendships can significantly reduce anxiety and depression among LGBTQ+ youth (Meyer, 2003).

In practical terms, Adin began to explore his identity more openly. He joined online forums, attended local LGBTQ+ meetups, and even participated in a few art projects that celebrated diversity. The more he surrounded himself with accepting individuals, the more he understood that his sexual orientation was not a flaw, but rather a facet of his vibrant identity.

Confronting Societal Norms

However, acceptance from friends didn't shield Adin from the harsh realities of a conservative town. The societal norms in Tarvel were rigid, and the fear of ostracism loomed large. Adin often found himself in situations where he had to navigate the treacherous waters of public opinion. For instance, during a high school assembly, a guest speaker denounced LGBTQ+ rights, claiming they were "against the natural order." Adin felt a mix of anger and despair, but Maya's unwavering support reminded him that he was not alone in this fight.

This experience highlighted the theory of *minority stress*, which posits that LGBTQ+ individuals face unique stressors due to their marginalized status. Adin learned to channel his frustration into activism, inspired by the acceptance he felt from Maya and others who stood by him.

The Transformation into Activism

With newfound courage, Adin decided to take action. He organized a small gathering in his backyard, inviting friends and allies to discuss LGBTQ+ rights and share their experiences. The event was a revelation; it was the first time many of them had openly discussed their identities without fear. The laughter, the tears, and the solidarity formed a bond that Adin had only dreamed of before.

This grassroots effort laid the groundwork for what would become a larger movement within Tarvel. Adin's journey from a closeted teenager to a budding activist was fueled by the simple yet profound acceptance of a friend. As he often reflected, "If Maya could see me for who I truly am, then maybe the world could too."

Conclusion: The Importance of Acceptance

In retrospect, the acceptance from Maya was not just a personal triumph for Adin; it was a reminder of the importance of allyship in the LGBTQ+ community. Acceptance can be a powerful tool for change, allowing individuals to embrace their true selves and inspire others to do the same. Adin's story illustrates that sometimes, all it takes is one person to change everything.

As he continued his journey toward activism, Adin carried with him the lessons learned from that pivotal moment of acceptance. He became determined to be that person for others, understanding that the fight for LGBTQ+ rights was not just a battle for legislation, but a profound struggle for love, understanding, and acceptance in every corner of the world.

$$\text{Acceptance} + \text{Support} = \text{Empowerment} \tag{5}$$

In conclusion, Adin Xeris's life was forever altered by the power of acceptance, proving that in a world filled with barriers, the simplest act of love can pave the way for monumental change.

Discovering the LGBTQ Community

As Adin navigated the tumultuous waters of adolescence in Tarvel, a small town steeped in conservative values, he found himself grappling with feelings of isolation and confusion regarding his sexual orientation. It was during this period of self-discovery that he stumbled upon the vibrant, albeit hidden, LGBTQ community that existed within the shadows of his hometown. This discovery would not only shape his identity but also ignite the fire of activism that would define his future.

The Hidden Network

The LGBTQ community in Tarvel was not overt; it was a clandestine network of individuals who, like Adin, sought connection and acceptance in a world that often marginalized them. This community operated under the radar, meeting in secret locations—basements, back rooms of cafes, and even in the secluded corners of local parks. The thrill of these clandestine gatherings was akin to a speakeasy during Prohibition; a place where one could shed the weight of societal expectations and be their true selves.

Adin's first encounter with this community came through a friend he had met in high school, who, after much hesitation, revealed their own identity and extended an invitation to a gathering. This was a pivotal moment for Adin; it was the first time he felt the warmth of belonging. The experience was electric—filled with laughter, shared stories of struggle, and an unspoken understanding that they were all in this together.

Theoretical Framework: Social Identity Theory

To understand the significance of Adin's discovery, we can apply *Social Identity Theory* (Tajfel & Turner, 1979), which posits that an individual's self-concept is derived from their perceived membership in social groups. For Adin, discovering the LGBTQ community allowed him to reshape his identity from one of isolation to one of solidarity. He began to see himself not just as a closeted teenager but as part of a larger movement—a community that celebrated diversity and fought against oppression.

This theory highlights the importance of group membership in fostering self-esteem and resilience. As Adin engaged with the community, he found strength in shared experiences and collective identity. The community provided him with a safe space to explore his sexuality and confront the fears that had long held him captive.

Challenges Faced

However, the path to acceptance was not without its challenges. The LGBTQ community in Tarvel faced significant external pressures, including harassment from conservative groups and societal stigma. Members often had to navigate a minefield of discrimination, which made the act of coming out a perilous endeavor.

Adin witnessed firsthand the struggles of his peers—some faced rejection from their families, while others dealt with violence and intimidation.

One poignant example was that of a close friend who, after bravely coming out to their parents, was met with hostility and disownment. This incident served as a stark reminder of the risks associated with being true to oneself in an unaccepting environment. Adin understood that while the community provided support, the external societal pressures could not be ignored.

Building a Safe Space

In response to these challenges, Adin and his peers took it upon themselves to create a safe space within their community. They organized informal meet-ups that evolved into more structured gatherings, where they could discuss their experiences, share resources, and strategize on how to combat discrimination. This initiative was crucial in fostering a sense of empowerment and solidarity among members.

Through these gatherings, Adin learned the importance of advocacy. They began to discuss the need for visibility and representation, recognizing that the more they shared their stories, the more they could challenge the stereotypes and misconceptions that plagued the LGBTQ community. This led to the formation of a local LGBTQ alliance, which aimed to provide education, support, and outreach to those still struggling with their identities.

The Power of Representation

Adin's discovery of the LGBTQ community not only transformed his personal life but also sparked a desire to advocate for broader societal change. He realized that representation mattered; seeing others live authentically encouraged him to embrace his own identity. This concept aligns with the *Contact Hypothesis* (Allport, 1954), which suggests that increased contact between different social groups can reduce prejudice and discrimination. By actively participating in the LGBTQ community, Adin hoped to foster understanding and acceptance within Tarvel.

The community organized events that showcased LGBTQ art, literature, and history, aiming to educate the broader public about the richness of LGBTQ experiences. These initiatives were met with mixed reactions; while some embraced the changes, others resisted, leading to heated debates and protests. Adin found himself at the forefront of these discussions, advocating for the rights and recognition of LGBTQ individuals in Tarvel.

Conclusion

Ultimately, discovering the LGBTQ community was a transformative experience for Adin. It provided him with a sense of belonging and a platform to express his identity. The challenges he faced alongside his peers only fueled his determination to fight for equality. This newfound community not only shaped his personal journey but also laid the groundwork for his future activism, as he emerged from the shadows of Tarvel, ready to battle for LGBTQ freedom.

Adin's journey illustrates the power of community in the face of adversity and highlights the importance of creating safe spaces for marginalized individuals. It is a testament to the resilience of the human spirit and the transformative impact of connection and solidarity in the fight for justice.

Adin's Decision to Fight for Equality

In the quaint yet conservative town of Tarvel, where the whispers of disapproval echoed louder than the voices of acceptance, Adin Xeris found himself at a crossroads. The moment he realized that he was not just different but also deserving of love and respect, a spark ignited within him—a spark that would soon transform into a roaring fire of activism. It was not merely the personal struggle of coming out that propelled Adin into the world of LGBTQ advocacy; it was the collective pain of those around him, the stories of discrimination, and the longing for equality that galvanized his resolve.

Theoretical Framework: Identity and Activism

Adin's decision to fight for equality can be understood through the lens of social identity theory, which posits that individuals derive a sense of self from their group memberships. For Adin, identifying as a member of the LGBTQ community was not just a personal revelation; it was a collective awakening. According to Tajfel and Turner (1979), individuals strive to maintain a positive social identity, and when faced with prejudice, they are often motivated to engage in activism to improve the status of their group. Adin was no exception.

As he navigated the complexities of his identity, he came to realize that his struggles were not isolated incidents but part of a broader systemic issue. The discriminatory practices embedded within the fabric of Tarvel's society were not just personal affronts; they were societal injustices that demanded attention. Adin felt a moral obligation to challenge these injustices, a sentiment echoed by many activists who have come before him.

The Problems at Hand

The decision to fight for equality was not without its challenges. Adin faced a plethora of issues, including:

- **Social Stigmatization:** The fear of rejection from family and friends loomed large. Adin often recalled the conversations he overheard in the school hallways—jokes about "fags" and "dykes" that were meant to be humorous but cut deeper than any knife. These experiences fostered a sense of isolation, yet they also fueled his desire to create a more inclusive environment.

- **Institutional Barriers:** The legal landscape in Tarvel was fraught with obstacles. Laws prohibiting same-sex marriage and anti-discrimination measures created an atmosphere of fear and uncertainty. Adin understood that to effect real change, he would need to confront these institutional barriers head-on.

- **Internalized Homophobia:** Like many LGBTQ individuals, Adin grappled with internalized homophobia—the internal conflict that arises when societal norms clash with personal identity. This struggle manifested in moments of self-doubt, yet it also served as a catalyst for his activism. Adin learned that confronting these feelings was not just essential for his own well-being but for the well-being of others who felt similarly trapped.

Examples of Inspiration

Adin's journey was influenced by numerous figures in the LGBTQ rights movement. He found inspiration in the stories of activists like Harvey Milk, whose courage in the face of adversity resonated with his own experiences. Milk's famous quote, "You gotta give them hope," became a mantra for Adin. He realized that fighting for equality was not just about changing laws; it was about changing hearts and minds.

Additionally, the Stonewall Riots of 1969 served as a historical touchstone for Adin. The bravery of those who fought back against oppression during that pivotal moment in history illuminated the path forward. Adin often reflected on the courage it took for those individuals to stand up and say, "Enough is enough!" This historical context provided a framework for understanding the importance of collective action and solidarity in the fight for LGBTQ rights.

The Moment of Decision

It was during a particularly poignant moment at a local LGBTQ gathering that Adin made his decision to actively engage in the fight for equality. Surrounded by individuals who shared their stories of hardship and resilience, he felt an overwhelming sense of belonging. The realization that he was not alone in his struggles ignited a passion within him.

Adin stood up, heart racing, and shared his own story—a tale of fear, acceptance, and the desire for change. The room erupted in applause, and in that moment, Adin understood the power of vulnerability. It was a turning point; he decided then and there that he would not only advocate for himself but for everyone who had been silenced by fear and discrimination.

Conclusion

Adin's decision to fight for equality was a culmination of personal experiences, theoretical understanding, and a profound sense of community. It was a journey marked by struggle, inspiration, and a relentless pursuit of justice. As he stepped into the role of an activist, he carried with him the weight of his experiences and the hope of a brighter future for all. His resolve to challenge the status quo and advocate for LGBTQ rights would lay the groundwork for a movement that sought to dismantle the barriers of prejudice and create a more inclusive society.

In the words of Audre Lorde, "I am not free while any woman is unfree, even when her shackles are very different from my own." Adin embraced this philosophy, recognizing that the fight for equality was not just a personal endeavor but a collective responsibility. And with that understanding, he embarked on a journey that would forever change the landscape of Tarvel and beyond.

The Birth of Adin Xeris, the Activist

In the small, conservative town of Tarvel, where whispers often carried more weight than shouts, the transformation of Adin Xeris from a timid teenager grappling with his identity into a fierce activist was not merely a personal journey; it was a social awakening. This metamorphosis marked a pivotal moment not only in Adin's life but also in the fabric of Tarvel's society, which had long been woven with threads of traditional values and unyielding norms.

The Catalyst for Change

Adin's awakening began with a simple yet profound realization: he was not alone. In the midst of his internal struggles, a friend—a vibrant, unapologetic member of the LGBTQ community—extended a hand of acceptance that Adin had desperately needed. This friendship served as the catalyst for his activism. It was a moment of clarity that illuminated the path ahead, revealing the stark contrast between the oppressive silence of his upbringing and the liberating chorus of voices advocating for change.

$$C = \frac{F}{A} \tag{6}$$

Where C represents the catalyst for change, F is the force of acceptance from peers, and A is the area of influence within the community. This equation illustrates how the acceptance from one individual can exponentially increase the potential for activism within a marginalized community.

The First Steps into Activism

Fueled by newfound courage, Adin began attending underground LGBTQ gatherings, where the air was thick with both fear and hope. These clandestine meetings were a stark contrast to the fear-laden environment of Tarvel. Here, Adin found a community that not only understood his struggles but also shared his vision for equality. The meetings were filled with laughter, tears, and the kind of discussions that ignited a fire in Adin's heart.

It was during one of these gatherings that Adin first spoke out publicly about his experiences. He shared stories of the pain of hiding, the fear of rejection, and the hope for a future where love was not dictated by societal norms. This moment was crucial; it was the first time he felt the power of his voice and the impact it could have on others.

Facing Opposition

However, the journey was not without its challenges. As Adin's voice grew louder, so did the opposition from conservative groups in Tarvel. The backlash was swift and brutal. Flyers were circulated, calling for a boycott of any event that included LGBTQ individuals, and Adin received threats that made him question his safety. Yet, rather than retreating into silence, these threats only fueled his determination.

Adin understood that activism was not merely about visibility; it was about resilience. He began to study the theory of social movements, particularly the works of scholars like Charles Tilly, who emphasized the importance of collective action in effecting social change. Tilly's framework provided Adin with the theoretical backbone to understand the dynamics of power and resistance.

$$R = P \cdot E \qquad (7)$$

Where R is the resistance faced, P is the power of the opposition, and E is the effectiveness of the activist's strategies. Adin realized that while the power of the opposition was formidable, the effectiveness of his strategies—community organizing, public speaking, and coalition-building—could counteract it.

Creating a Platform for Change

With a growing network of allies, Adin took the next step: creating a platform for LGBTQ voices in Tarvel. He organized the first LGBTQ Awareness March, a bold declaration of existence in a town that had long silenced its queer population. The march was a spectacle of color and pride, drawing attention from local media and igniting conversations across the community.

The event was not just a protest; it was a celebration of identity. Adin's speeches resonated with both supporters and skeptics, as he eloquently articulated the need for acceptance and equality. He used humor and storytelling, reminiscent of the comedic styles of Dave Chappelle, to engage the audience and dismantle preconceived notions about LGBTQ individuals.

$$E = \frac{S + H}{C} \qquad (8)$$

Where E is the effectiveness of the message, S is the storytelling component, H is the humor used to engage the audience, and C is the complexity of the issues being addressed. Adin's ability to simplify complex issues through relatable narratives was key to his success.

The Emergence of a Leader

As Adin continued to advocate for LGBTQ rights, he emerged as a leader in the community. His passion and dedication attracted attention from national LGBTQ organizations, leading to invitations to speak at conferences and events. Each appearance was an opportunity to amplify the voices of those who had been silenced for too long.

Adin's journey from a closeted youth to a prominent activist was not just about personal growth; it was about the birth of a movement. His experiences mirrored those of countless others who had faced similar struggles, and through his activism, he became a beacon of hope for many.

Conclusion

The birth of Adin Xeris, the activist, was a testament to the power of acceptance, resilience, and the unwavering belief in the right to love freely. His story serves as a reminder that activism often begins with a single voice, one that dares to speak out against injustice, and in doing so, inspires a chorus of others to join the fight for equality. As Adin would later reflect, "Activism isn't just about changing laws; it's about changing hearts and minds—one laugh, one story, and one march at a time."

The Impact of Adin's Supportive Family

In the journey of any activist, the role of family can be a double-edged sword. For Adin Xeris, his family's unwavering support became the bedrock of his activism. This section explores the profound impact of Adin's supportive family, providing insight into how familial acceptance not only shaped his identity but also fueled his fight for LGBTQ rights in Tarvel.

The Foundation of Acceptance

Adin's family, while rooted in conservative values typical of Tarvel, exhibited a remarkable ability to adapt and embrace change. Acceptance in the family context can be understood through the lens of *family systems theory*, which posits that individuals are influenced by the dynamics within their family unit. Adin's parents, recognizing their child's struggles, chose to engage in open conversations about sexuality and identity. This choice was pivotal, as it created a safe space for Adin to express his fears and aspirations.

$$\text{Supportive Family Dynamics} = \text{Open Communication} + \text{Unconditional Love} \tag{9}$$

This equation emphasizes that the combination of open communication and unconditional love leads to supportive family dynamics, which in Adin's case, was instrumental in his development as an activist.

Navigating Conservative Values

Despite their initial conservative beliefs, Adin's family demonstrated a willingness to evolve. This transformation can be analyzed through the *stages of change model*, which outlines how individuals and families progress through stages from pre-contemplation to maintenance. Adin's parents moved from a place of pre-contemplation, where they held traditional views about sexuality, to contemplation and ultimately to acceptance.

Stages of Change = Pre-contemplation → Contemplation → Acceptance (10)

This journey not only illustrates the challenges faced by families but also highlights the potential for growth and understanding. Adin's experience showcases how families can become allies in the fight for equality, even when starting from a place of misunderstanding.

Empowerment Through Support

The emotional support provided by Adin's family was not just a passive acceptance; it actively empowered him to embrace his identity and advocate for others. Research indicates that individuals with supportive family structures are more likely to engage in positive social activism. For Adin, this support translated into a fierce commitment to LGBTQ rights, as he often recounted the moments of encouragement from his family during his early struggles.

Empowerment = Support × Identity Affirmation (11)

This formula encapsulates the idea that empowerment is a product of both support and identity affirmation, both of which were abundant in Adin's familial interactions.

The Ripple Effect of Support

Adin's family's support extended beyond their home. It created a ripple effect within the community, encouraging other families to accept their LGBTQ children. This phenomenon can be understood through the concept of *social contagion*, where behaviors and norms are spread through social networks. As Adin became more vocal about his identity and activism, his family's acceptance inspired others to follow suit.

Social Change = Individual Actions × Community Support (12)

In this context, Adin's individual actions, bolstered by his family's support, contributed significantly to broader community acceptance of LGBTQ individuals in Tarvel.

Conclusion: A Legacy of Love

In conclusion, the impact of Adin's supportive family cannot be overstated. Their journey from conservative values to unconditional acceptance exemplifies the transformative power of love and understanding. Adin's activism was deeply rooted in the belief that everyone deserves to be loved and accepted for who they are, a belief that was instilled in him by his family.

As Tarvel continues to evolve, the legacy of Adin's family serves as a beacon of hope, demonstrating that change is possible when families choose love over prejudice. Adin Xeris' story is not just one of personal triumph; it is a testament to the power of family support in the fight for LGBTQ rights.

$$\text{Legacy of Activism} = \text{Family Support} + \text{Community Acceptance} \qquad (13)$$

This final equation summarizes the essential components of Adin's legacy, emphasizing that the intersection of family support and community acceptance is crucial in the ongoing struggle for equality and justice.

The Battle Begins

The Battle Begins

The Battle Begins

The moment Adin Xeris stepped into the local LGBTQ community in Tarvel, it was as if he had walked into a scene from a Dave Chappelle skit—awkward, hilarious, and filled with a sense of urgency. This was not just about finding acceptance; it was about creating a revolution in a town that had been more closed than a clam at low tide.

Finding Like-Minded Individuals in Tarvel

Adin quickly discovered that he was not alone. Tarvel, despite its conservative undercurrents, had pockets of individuals who shared his vision for equality. They were a ragtag group of misfits, artists, and activists—each with their own stories of struggle and resilience. It was in these meetings that Adin found his voice, often punctuated by laughter and camaraderie, reminiscent of a Chappelle comedy special where humor was the weapon against oppression.

Organizing Underground LGBTQ Gatherings

The gatherings started small, often held in the backrooms of local cafes or the basements of sympathetic allies. Adin and his newfound friends would gather to share experiences, strategize, and plan events that would challenge the status quo. They coined the term "Tarvel Underground" for their clandestine meetings, a nod to the Prohibition-era speakeasies.

$$\text{Activism} = \text{Community} + \text{Strategy} + \text{Courage} \tag{14}$$

This equation became the mantra of the Tarvel Underground. The community provided the support, strategy was necessary for effective action, and courage was the fuel that propelled them forward.

Facing Opposition from Conservative Groups

However, with every action comes reaction. The conservative factions in Tarvel were not about to sit idly by while Adin and his crew stirred the pot. They rallied their forces, launching campaigns that painted the LGBTQ community as a threat to family values. Adin often likened their tactics to a bad comedy routine—predictable, tired, and lacking any real punchline.

Media Attention and Public Scrutiny

As the Tarvel Underground grew, so did the media attention. Local news outlets began to cover their gatherings, often sensationalizing the events. Adin learned quickly that media portrayal could either make or break a movement. He decided to take control of the narrative, utilizing social media platforms to share the truth about their mission.

$$\text{Narrative Control} = \frac{\text{Authenticity}}{\text{Media Sensationalism}} \tag{15}$$

This equation highlighted the delicate balance between maintaining authenticity and combating the sensationalism that often accompanied LGBTQ issues in the media.

Creating a Platform for LGBTQ Voices

Recognizing the need for a platform, Adin spearheaded the creation of a local LGBTQ newsletter. It became a beacon of hope, featuring stories of local heroes, upcoming events, and resources for those struggling with their identity. The newsletter was a hit—like finding a hidden gem in a thrift store.

The First LGBTQ Awareness March in Tarvel

The culmination of their efforts was the first LGBTQ Awareness March in Tarvel. Adin stood at the forefront, a mix of nerves and excitement bubbling within him. As they marched through the streets, holding signs and chanting slogans, it felt like they were rewriting the narrative of their town.

$$\text{March Success} = \text{Visibility} \times \text{Community Engagement} \qquad (16)$$

The march was not just about visibility; it was about engaging the community, sparking conversations that had long been avoided.

In the aftermath, Adin reflected on the journey thus far. The battle was just beginning, but with each step taken, they were dismantling the walls of ignorance and fear. He could feel the energy shift in Tarvel, and it was intoxicating.

The battle for LGBTQ freedom in Tarvel was not just a fight for rights; it was a fight for existence, identity, and the right to love freely. Adin Xeris was no longer just a name; he was becoming a symbol of hope and resilience in a world that often tried to silence voices like his.

And just like that, the battle began, not with a bang, but with the laughter of a community finding its voice, echoing the wisdom of Chappelle: sometimes, the best way to fight back is to laugh in the face of adversity.

Joining the Local LGBTQ Community

Finding like-minded individuals in Tarvel

In the quaint, conservative town of Tarvel, where the air was thick with tradition and the whispers of judgment echoed in every corner, Adin Xeris embarked on a quest that would change his life forever. This quest was not merely about self-discovery; it was about finding a community, a tribe of individuals who shared the same struggles, dreams, and aspirations. The journey of finding like-minded individuals in Tarvel was akin to searching for a needle in a haystack, but Adin was determined, armed with a heart full of hope and a spirit that refused to be crushed.

The Need for Connection

The first step in Adin's journey was recognizing the profound need for connection. In a society where conservative values often overshadowed personal identities, the fear of isolation loomed large. The theory of *social identity* posits that individuals derive a sense of self from their group memberships (Tajfel & Turner, 1979). For Adin, this meant seeking out others who identified as LGBTQ, individuals who would understand the complexities of his existence.

$$S = \frac{1}{N} \sum_{i=1}^{N} I_i \qquad (17)$$

Where S is the social identity strength, N is the number of group members, and I_i represents the individual identity contributions. Adin's quest was to amplify S by increasing N and fostering a sense of belonging.

The Underground Network

Adin soon discovered that Tarvel had an underground network of LGBTQ individuals, each hiding in the shadows, much like him. These were not just individuals; they were warriors in their own right, battling societal norms while seeking solace in each other's company. It was through social media platforms and encrypted messaging apps that Adin began to connect with others who shared his experiences.

The challenge, however, was immense. Many were reluctant to reveal their identities due to the fear of backlash from the conservative community. This phenomenon is often referred to as *the fear of coming out*, which can lead to feelings of isolation and anxiety (Meyer, 2003). Adin organized secret meetups in local cafes and parks, where laughter and camaraderie could flourish, albeit under the veil of secrecy.

Building Trust and Community

As the group began to form, the next crucial step was building trust. Adin understood that trust was the foundation of any community, particularly one that had to navigate the treacherous waters of societal rejection. He initiated icebreaker sessions, where members could share their stories, fears, and hopes in a safe environment.

$$T = \frac{C + R + S}{3} \tag{18}$$

Where T is the trust level, C is the level of communication, R is the level of respect, and S represents shared experiences. Adin's mission was to increase T by fostering open lines of communication, mutual respect, and the sharing of personal narratives.

The First Gathering

The first official gathering of the Tarvel LGBTQ community was a pivotal moment. It was held in a secluded backyard, adorned with fairy lights and rainbow flags. The atmosphere buzzed with anticipation and nervous energy. Adin stood at the forefront, heart racing, as he welcomed everyone.

"Tonight, we are not just individuals; we are a family," he proclaimed, his voice steady yet passionate. This gathering was not just about socializing; it was about empowerment. Adin introduced discussions on LGBTQ rights, mental health, and the importance of advocacy.

The impact was immediate; members began to share their stories, revealing the struggles they had faced in a town that often felt hostile. The room filled with laughter, tears, and a sense of belonging that many had never experienced before.

Challenges Ahead

However, the road ahead was fraught with challenges. As the community grew, so did the scrutiny from conservative groups. The theory of *in-group vs. out-group dynamics* (Tajfel, 1982) became evident as the LGBTQ community found itself increasingly at odds with the prevailing societal norms. Adin and his newfound friends had to navigate hostility and discrimination, which often manifested in the form of hate speech and protests.

The Power of Solidarity

Despite these challenges, the power of solidarity became the bedrock of Adin's activism. The community began to organize events that not only served to unite them but also to educate the broader Tarvel population about LGBTQ issues. The first public awareness event was a small but significant step.

$$E = \sum_{j=1}^{M} P_j \tag{19}$$

Where E represents the event's effectiveness, M is the number of participants, and P_j is the positive impact of each participant's involvement. Adin believed that by increasing M, they could amplify their message and create a ripple effect in Tarvel.

Conclusion

Finding like-minded individuals in Tarvel was not merely about forming a social group; it was about creating a movement. Adin Xeris understood that in a world that often sought to divide, they had the power to unite. Through trust, connection, and shared experiences, they began to carve out a space where love and acceptance could thrive. This was just the beginning of a long and arduous journey, but Adin was ready to lead the charge, armed with the knowledge that he was not alone in his fight for equality.

Organizing underground LGBTQ gatherings

In the conservative enclave of Tarvel, where the air was thick with social expectations and the scent of unspoken truths, Adin Xeris found himself at the forefront of a clandestine movement. The idea was simple yet radical: to create safe spaces for LGBTQ individuals to gather, share their experiences, and build community, all while dodging the watchful eyes of those who would rather see them silenced.

The Need for Safe Spaces

The necessity for underground gatherings stemmed from the oppressive environment that characterized Tarvel. As Adin observed, "We were living in a town where being yourself felt like a crime." This sentiment resonated with many, leading to a collective yearning for a sanctuary where authenticity could flourish.

$$S = \frac{E}{C} \tag{20}$$

Where S represents the safety of the gathering, E is the emotional support provided, and C is the conservativeness of the environment. The equation illustrates that as the emotional support increases, the safety of the gathering exponentially rises, even in the face of a conservative backdrop.

Challenges of Organization

Organizing these gatherings was not without its challenges. The first problem was logistics. Finding a location that was both discreet and accessible required creativity and, often, a network of trusted allies. Adin and his friends would scout out abandoned warehouses, basements of sympathetic businesses, or even backyards of those willing to lend a hand.

"Getting a group together was like planning a heist," Adin recalled. "You had to be stealthy, and everyone had to be on the same page."

Recruiting Participants

The next hurdle was recruitment. Flyers were out of the question, and social media was a double-edged sword—great for spreading the word but also a potential trap. Instead, Adin relied on word-of-mouth and coded language in casual conversations.

- **Example 1:** "Hey, you know that coffee shop on Main Street? They have a great book club on Thursdays."

- **Example 2:** "I heard there's a cool art show happening this weekend, maybe we can check it out together?"

These seemingly innocuous invitations would lead to discussions about upcoming gatherings, allowing participants to gauge each other's comfort levels before revealing the true nature of the event.

Creating an Inclusive Atmosphere

Once the gatherings commenced, Adin emphasized the importance of inclusivity. The underground meetings were designed to be welcoming to everyone, regardless of their sexual orientation or gender identity. "We wanted to create a space where people felt they could express themselves without judgment," Adin explained.

This commitment to inclusivity manifested in various ways:

- **Workshops:** Hosting workshops on topics like self-acceptance, mental health, and advocacy helped attendees feel empowered.

- **Support Circles:** These circles allowed individuals to share their stories and connect on a deeper level, fostering a sense of belonging.

- **Art and Expression:** Encouraging participants to showcase their art, poetry, and music provided an outlet for creativity and self-expression.

Navigating Opposition

Despite the positive impact of these gatherings, opposition was inevitable. Conservative groups began to take notice, often disrupting events or attempting to intimidate attendees. Adin and his team had to develop strategies to mitigate these threats, such as:

- **Safety Protocols:** Establishing clear protocols for what to do in case of an intrusion, including designated escape routes and safe words.

- **Legal Support:** Building relationships with local LGBTQ-friendly lawyers to ensure participants knew their rights.

Adin recalled a particularly tense gathering where a group of protestors attempted to storm the venue. "We had to lock the doors and call the police," he said. "But it only made us more determined to keep going."

The Impact of Underground Gatherings

The underground gatherings not only provided immediate support but also laid the groundwork for broader activism. As participants left these safe spaces, they carried with them a renewed sense of purpose and community. Many went on to become advocates themselves, inspired by their experiences and the connections they forged.

$$I = P \times R \tag{21}$$

Where I is the impact of the gatherings, P is the number of participants, and R is the rate of engagement in activism post-gathering. This equation highlights that as the number of participants increases and their engagement rises, the overall impact of these gatherings expands exponentially.

Conclusion

In summary, organizing underground LGBTQ gatherings in Tarvel was a labor of love, fraught with challenges but ultimately transformative. Adin Xeris and his allies turned fear into fellowship, creating a ripple effect that would change the fabric of their community. These gatherings were not just meetings; they were acts of rebellion, affirmations of identity, and the seeds of a movement that would grow far beyond the shadows of Tarvel.

As Adin famously said, "We were not just surviving; we were thriving, and we were ready to fight for our place in the light."

Facing opposition from conservative groups

As Adin Xeris began to gain momentum within the LGBTQ community in Tarvel, the backlash from conservative groups grew increasingly vocal and organized. This opposition manifested in various forms, from public protests to attempts at legislative sabotage, creating a challenging environment for Adin and his allies.

The first major instance of opposition came during the planning stages of the inaugural LGBTQ Awareness March in Tarvel. Conservative groups, led by the local chapter of the "Family Values Coalition," launched a campaign to discredit the event. They utilized a mix of misinformation and fear tactics, claiming that the march would promote "immorality" and "corrupt the youth" of Tarvel. This narrative was steeped in the historical context of how LGBTQ movements have often been framed by conservative ideologies.

Opposition Intensity $= f$(Public Sentiment, Media Coverage, Political Climate)

(22)

Where: - Public Sentiment is the general attitude of the community towards LGBTQ rights. - Media Coverage reflects how local and national media portray the events. - Political Climate indicates the stance of local government and influential political figures.

The backlash intensified as the march date approached. Conservative groups organized counter-protests, often outnumbering LGBTQ supporters, which fueled a sense of fear among participants. Adin, however, remained undeterred. He recognized that this opposition was not merely a local issue but part of a broader ideological battle. The conservative narrative was rooted in a longstanding tradition of opposing social change, often relying on religious rhetoric and a perceived moral high ground.

One prominent example of this opposition was a pamphlet distributed by the Family Values Coalition, which featured inflammatory language and misleading statistics about LGBTQ individuals. The pamphlet claimed that "the normalization of homosexuality leads to increased rates of disease and moral decay." Such claims were not only unfounded but also echoed a historical pattern of stigmatization that LGBTQ activists had been fighting against for decades.

In response to these tactics, Adin and his team engaged in a strategic communication campaign aimed at countering the misinformation. They organized community forums to educate the public about LGBTQ issues, emphasizing the importance of acceptance and understanding. They also reached out to local media outlets to share their perspective and correct false narratives. This proactive approach helped to shift public sentiment gradually, as more residents began to recognize the value of inclusivity and diversity.

Despite these efforts, the opposition remained fierce. Conservative groups began to lobby local government officials to enact ordinances that would restrict the rights of LGBTQ individuals. For instance, they proposed a "bathroom bill" that would require individuals to use public restrooms corresponding to their sex assigned at birth, a move that many activists viewed as a direct attack on transgender rights.

The tension reached a boiling point during a city council meeting where Adin was invited to speak. The meeting was packed, with supporters and opponents alike. Adin, armed with data and personal stories, addressed the council, articulating the need for equality and the harmful effects of discrimination.

However, he faced a barrage of heckling from conservative attendees, illustrating the deep divisions within the community.

$$\text{Community Division} = \frac{\text{Supporters} - \text{Opponents}}{\text{Total Population}} \tag{23}$$

Where: - Supporters refers to those in favor of LGBTQ rights. - Opponents indicates those against it. - Total Population is the overall number of individuals in Tarvel.

This equation highlights the stark reality that, while Adin was rallying support, the opposition was equally organized and motivated.

In the face of such challenges, Adin found strength in solidarity. He strengthened alliances with other marginalized groups, recognizing that the fight for LGBTQ rights was intertwined with broader social justice movements. This coalition-building became a critical strategy in countering the conservative narrative, showcasing that the struggle for equality was not just an LGBTQ issue but a human rights issue.

Ultimately, the opposition from conservative groups served to galvanize the LGBTQ community in Tarvel. Rather than deterring activism, it ignited a fire within Adin and his allies, leading to a more robust and united front. The challenges they faced became a rallying cry, inspiring countless individuals to join the fight for equality and justice.

As the LGBTQ Awareness March approached, the opposition's efforts only served to highlight the necessity of the event. Adin's determination and resilience became emblematic of a larger movement, one that would not back down in the face of adversity. This chapter in Adin's journey illustrated that while opposition may be formidable, the power of community and the pursuit of justice can ultimately prevail.

Media attention and public scrutiny

As Adin Xeris began to gain traction as a leading figure in the fight for LGBTQ rights in Tarvel, the media attention surrounding his activism intensified. This spotlight, while providing a platform for advocacy, also brought with it a wave of public scrutiny that tested Adin's resilience and commitment to the cause. The relationship between media representation and public perception is a complex one, often oscillating between empowerment and vilification.

The Role of Media in Activism

Media plays a pivotal role in shaping public discourse around social issues. According to McCombs and Shaw's agenda-setting theory, the media doesn't just tell us what to think, but rather what to think about. In Adin's case, the local and national media began to highlight LGBTQ issues in Tarvel, framing them as a significant social concern. This increased visibility was essential in bringing awareness to the struggles faced by the LGBTQ community.

However, media attention can be a double-edged sword. While it can amplify voices and bring issues to the forefront, it can also distort narratives. Adin found himself at the center of sensational headlines that often prioritized drama over substance. For instance, a local newspaper once ran a story titled, "The Rise of the Rainbow Warrior: Is Tarvel Ready for Change?" While the article did cover important aspects of Adin's activism, it also sensationalized his personal life, focusing on his relationships and public appearances rather than the pressing issues of discrimination and inequality.

Public Scrutiny and Its Challenges

With increased media attention came heightened public scrutiny. Adin quickly learned that every action he took was under the microscope. Social media platforms became battlegrounds for opinions, both supportive and hostile. Adin faced backlash from conservative groups, who utilized media channels to spread misinformation and foster a narrative that painted him as a radical disruptor of traditional values.

For instance, a widely circulated video clip of Adin speaking at a local LGBTQ gathering was edited to misrepresent his comments. Critics claimed he advocated for the "indoctrination" of youth, a term that resonated deeply with conservative audiences. This misrepresentation led to protests outside his events, with signs reading "Protect Our Children from Adin Xeris!" Such incidents exemplified the challenges activists face when their messages are distorted, leading to public misunderstanding and fear.

Navigating the Media Landscape

To combat the negative narratives, Adin and his team recognized the importance of proactive media engagement. They organized press conferences, invited journalists to LGBTQ events, and utilized social media to share authentic stories from the community. By doing so, Adin aimed to create a counter-narrative that focused on the positive impact of LGBTQ advocacy.

One successful campaign involved sharing personal testimonials from community members about how Adin's activism had changed their lives. This humanizing approach helped shift the media narrative from one of fear to one of hope and resilience. Adin's ability to navigate this complex media landscape was crucial in maintaining momentum for the LGBTQ movement in Tarvel.

The Impact of Media Attention on Activism

The media attention that Adin garnered had significant implications for the LGBTQ movement in Tarvel. On one hand, it brought much-needed visibility to the cause, increasing participation in events and fostering a sense of community among supporters. The first LGBTQ Awareness March in Tarvel, which Adin helped organize, attracted hundreds of participants, largely due to the media coverage leading up to the event.

On the other hand, the scrutiny also led to increased pressure on Adin to perform and deliver results. Activists often face the burden of representation; their actions are viewed as reflections of the entire community. This phenomenon is well-documented in social movement theory, where the concept of "representative burden" suggests that activists bear the weight of ensuring their actions are perceived positively by the public.

Adin often felt this pressure acutely. He would joke with friends, saying, "I didn't sign up to be the poster child for LGBTQ rights; I just wanted to be me!" This humor masked the underlying stress of constant visibility and the fear of failure.

Conclusion

In conclusion, the media attention and public scrutiny surrounding Adin Xeris were critical components of his journey as an activist. While the media served as a vehicle for change, it also posed significant challenges that required strategic navigation. Adin's experiences illustrate the intricate dance between media representation and activism, highlighting the importance of authenticity, community engagement, and resilience in the face of adversity. As he continued his fight for equality, Adin learned that the media could be both a powerful ally and a formidable opponent, shaping the narrative of LGBTQ rights in Tarvel for years to come.

Creating a platform for LGBTQ voices

In the heart of Tarvel, Adin Xeris recognized a critical gap in the representation of LGBTQ voices within the community. The prevailing conservative values stifled open dialogue, and many individuals felt marginalized, voiceless, and isolated. Adin's commitment to activism was not merely about fighting for rights; it was about amplifying the voices of those who had been silenced. This section delves into the strategies Adin employed to create a platform for LGBTQ voices, addressing relevant theories, challenges faced, and examples that illustrate the impact of these efforts.

Theoretical Framework

Adin's approach to creating a platform for LGBTQ voices can be analyzed through the lens of **Critical Theory**, which advocates for the empowerment of marginalized groups by challenging dominant narratives and structures. This theory posits that social change can be achieved through the elevation of voices that have historically been silenced. Adin understood that the first step toward equality was to ensure that LGBTQ individuals in Tarvel had a space to express their experiences, struggles, and aspirations.

Moreover, the concept of **Intersectionality**, introduced by Kimberlé Crenshaw, became a guiding principle for Adin. Intersectionality emphasizes that individuals experience oppression in varying configurations and degrees of intensity based on multiple identities, including race, gender, sexuality, and class. By acknowledging the diverse backgrounds within the LGBTQ community, Adin aimed to create an inclusive platform that represented all voices, especially those of marginalized subgroups.

Challenges Faced

Creating a platform for LGBTQ voices in a conservative environment was fraught with challenges. One of the primary obstacles was the pervasive fear of backlash. Many individuals were hesitant to speak out due to concerns about discrimination, violence, or ostracization from their families and communities. Adin faced the daunting task of reassuring potential participants that their safety was paramount and that the community would stand together against any threats.

Additionally, there was the challenge of overcoming internalized homophobia and self-censorship. Many members of the LGBTQ community had internalized negative societal messages about their identities, leading to a reluctance to engage publicly. Adin understood that fostering an environment of acceptance and support was crucial for encouraging individuals to share their stories.

Strategies for Amplification

Adin initiated several strategies to create a platform for LGBTQ voices, which included:

- **Community Workshops:** Adin organized workshops aimed at educating LGBTQ individuals about their rights, self-advocacy, and storytelling techniques. These workshops provided a safe space for participants to share their experiences and learn from one another. The collective sharing fostered a sense of community and solidarity.

- **Social Media Campaigns:** Recognizing the power of digital platforms, Adin launched social media campaigns that encouraged individuals to share their stories using the hashtag #VoicesOfTarvel. This initiative not only amplified individual voices but also connected people across the region, creating a virtual community of support.

- **Public Forums and Open Mic Nights:** Adin facilitated public forums and open mic nights where LGBTQ individuals could speak openly about their experiences. These events attracted both supporters and skeptics, allowing for meaningful dialogue and the dismantling of stereotypes. The open mic nights became particularly popular, transforming into a vibrant celebration of identity and resilience.

- **Collaboration with Local Artists:** To further amplify voices, Adin collaborated with local artists to create visual art, poetry, and performances that reflected LGBTQ experiences. This artistic expression not only validated individual stories but also reached broader audiences, sparking conversations about LGBTQ issues in Tarvel.

Examples of Impact

One notable example of the impact of Adin's efforts was the **Tarvel Pride Festival,** an event that Adin helped organize. The festival featured speakers from the LGBTQ community, local artists, and workshops on various topics, including mental health and self-advocacy. The event drew an unprecedented crowd, showcasing the strength and diversity of the LGBTQ community in Tarvel.

Moreover, the social media campaign #VoicesOfTarvel gained traction, leading to increased visibility for LGBTQ issues. Stories shared online prompted local media coverage, shifting public perception and encouraging more individuals to come forward with their experiences. This newfound visibility played a crucial role in fostering a sense of belonging and empowerment among LGBTQ individuals in Tarvel.

Conclusion

Creating a platform for LGBTQ voices in Tarvel was a transformative endeavor led by Adin Xeris. Through strategic initiatives grounded in critical theory and intersectionality, Adin not only amplified individual stories but also fostered a sense of community and solidarity. Despite the challenges faced, the impact of these efforts was profound, leading to greater visibility, acceptance, and advocacy for LGBTQ rights in Tarvel. As Adin continued to champion these voices, the foundation for a more inclusive and equitable society began to take shape, inspiring future generations to carry the torch of activism forward.

The First LGBTQ Awareness March in Tarvel

In the heart of Tarvel, a small town with a big reputation for its conservative values, the winds of change began to stir as Adin Xeris and his fellow activists prepared for what would become a historic event: the First LGBTQ Awareness March. This was not just a walk in the park; it was a bold statement, a defiance of social norms, and a celebration of identity. The march aimed to raise awareness about LGBTQ issues, foster community solidarity, and challenge the prevailing prejudices that had long stifled voices in Tarvel.

The Planning Phase

Organizing the march was no easy feat. The team faced numerous challenges, ranging from securing permits to rallying participants. Adin and his allies understood that the success of the march depended on meticulous planning. They convened meetings in dimly lit basements, whispering about their plans like secret agents plotting a coup.

The first step was to establish a clear message. They decided on the slogan: "Love is Love, No Matter Where You Are!" This phrase encapsulated the essence of their struggle and resonated with the community's desire for acceptance. In mathematical terms, we can represent their goal as:

$$\text{Awareness} = \frac{\text{Unity} + \text{Visibility}}{\text{Fear}}$$

where **Awareness** is the outcome they sought, **Unity** represents the collective strength of the LGBTQ community, **Visibility** denotes the public presence during the march, and **Fear** is the societal stigma they aimed to diminish.

Mobilizing the Community

Adin and his team took to social media, using platforms like Facebook and Twitter to spread the word. They created eye-catching graphics and shared personal stories that highlighted the struggles faced by LGBTQ individuals in Tarvel. The campaign was met with mixed reactions. While many rallied to support the cause, others expressed outrage, fearing that the march would tarnish the town's reputation.

The tension in the air was palpable. Adin recalled the moment he received a threatening message from a local conservative group, warning him to cancel the event. Instead of cowering in fear, he used it as fuel. He posted the message online, turning the threat into a rallying cry: "If you're afraid of our love, imagine how strong it must be!"

The Day of the March

On the day of the march, the streets of Tarvel were alive with color and energy. Participants donned rainbow attire, waved flags, and carried signs that read, "Equality for All!" and "We Are Here, We Are Queer!" The atmosphere was electric, a stark contrast to the silence that often surrounded LGBTQ issues in the town.

Adin stood at the front of the procession, his heart racing. He took a moment to reflect on the journey that had brought them here. The march was not just about LGBTQ rights; it was about human rights. It was about the right to love freely, to express oneself without fear, and to exist authentically in a world that often demanded conformity.

Facing Opposition

However, the march was not without its challenges. As the participants made their way through the streets, they encountered a counter-protest organized by local conservative groups. These individuals held signs that read, "Protect Our Children!" and "God Says No!" The tension escalated, and for a moment, it seemed as if the march might devolve into chaos.

Adin, however, remained calm. He remembered the lessons he had learned about non-violence and the power of peaceful protest. He urged the marchers to continue forward, chanting affirmations of love and acceptance. They responded with unity, drowning out the opposition with chants of "Love Wins!"

This moment became a pivotal point in the march, exemplifying the strength of the LGBTQ community in the face of adversity. The equation of resilience can be expressed as:

$$\text{Resilience} = \text{Courage} \times \text{Solidarity}$$

where **Courage** is the individual bravery of each participant, and **Solidarity** is the collective support of the community.

Media Attention and Aftermath

As the march concluded, local media outlets began to take notice. News crews arrived, capturing the vibrant scenes and interviewing participants. For the first time, LGBTQ voices were given a platform in Tarvel. Adin's speech at the end of the march resonated deeply, as he called for continued activism and support for one another.

The aftermath of the march was transformative. It sparked conversations in homes, schools, and local businesses. People began to question their preconceived notions about LGBTQ individuals, and many conservative residents found themselves grappling with their beliefs.

In the following weeks, Tarvel witnessed a shift in public perception. Local businesses began to display pride flags, and discussions about LGBTQ rights emerged in town hall meetings. The march had ignited a flame of awareness that could not be extinguished.

Conclusion

The First LGBTQ Awareness March in Tarvel was more than just an event; it was a turning point in the fight for equality. Adin Xeris and his fellow activists proved that even in the most conservative of environments, love and acceptance could thrive. The march laid the groundwork for future activism, inspiring a new generation to advocate for their rights.

In the words of Adin, "We may have started with a whisper, but now our voices echo through the streets of Tarvel, and we will not be silenced!"

Thus, the legacy of the march continued to resonate, reminding everyone that the fight for LGBTQ rights is not just a local issue but a global struggle for justice and equality. The march in Tarvel was a testament to the power of community, courage, and the unwavering belief that love conquers all.

Adin Becomes a Leading Activist

Becoming the face of LGBTQ liberation

In the small, conservative town of Tarvel, where the air was thick with tradition and the whispers of disapproval echoed louder than the voices of acceptance, Adin Xeris emerged as a beacon of hope for the LGBTQ community. The journey to becoming the face of LGBTQ liberation was not merely a personal evolution; it was a collective struggle against the oppressive norms that had long dictated the lives of many.

The Weight of Representation

Adin understood the weight of representation. He was not just fighting for his identity; he was becoming the embodiment of a movement. In a society that often silenced marginalized voices, Adin's emergence was akin to a phoenix rising from the ashes. His visibility challenged the status quo, forcing the community to confront its own prejudices and biases.

The theory of *social representation* posits that individuals are influenced by the images and narratives they encounter in society. Adin's presence in the public sphere served as a counter-narrative to the stereotypical portrayals of LGBTQ individuals. By presenting himself authentically, he shattered the misconceptions that had long plagued the community.

$$R = f(P, E) \tag{24}$$

where R is representation, P is personal identity, and E is environmental context. Adin's personal identity, shaped by his experiences in Tarvel, was instrumental in redefining the environmental context in which LGBTQ issues were discussed.

Challenges of Visibility

However, visibility came with its own set of challenges. Adin faced immense pressure from both his supporters and detractors. The conservative factions in Tarvel were quick to mobilize against him, labeling him as a radical and a threat to traditional values. This backlash was not just a personal attack; it was an attack on the very essence of LGBTQ liberation.

Adin's decision to step into the limelight meant that he had to navigate a treacherous landscape of public opinion. He often found himself at the center of heated debates, with his every word scrutinized and analyzed. The psychological toll of such scrutiny cannot be understated. According to the theory of *impression management,* individuals in the public eye are constantly aware of how they are perceived and often modify their behavior to influence that perception.

$$I = \frac{P}{C} \tag{25}$$

where I is impression, P is performance, and C is context. Adin's performance as an activist was often shaped by the context of the backlash he faced, forcing him to balance authenticity with the need for acceptance.

Building a Movement

Despite the challenges, Adin's charisma and determination resonated with many. He began to attract attention not just locally, but nationally. His speeches at rallies and conferences inspired countless individuals to join the fight for LGBTQ rights. Adin leveraged social media to amplify his message, transforming from a local figure to a national icon.

The concept of *collective identity* played a crucial role in this transformation. By fostering a sense of belonging among LGBTQ individuals, Adin galvanized a movement that transcended geographical boundaries. He created a platform where voices that had long been silenced could be heard, fostering solidarity among diverse groups within the LGBTQ spectrum.

$$C = \sum_{i=1}^{n} I_i \tag{26}$$

where C is collective identity and I_i represents the individual identities within the movement. Adin's ability to unify these identities under a common cause was pivotal in establishing a robust activist community.

The Ripple Effect

Adin's rise as the face of LGBTQ liberation in Tarvel had a ripple effect that extended far beyond the town's borders. His activism inspired similar movements in other conservative regions, proving that change was possible even in the most unlikely places.

As he stood before crowds, rallying for equality, Adin became a symbol of resilience. His journey illustrated that the fight for LGBTQ rights was not just a local issue; it was a global struggle for human dignity and acceptance. The challenges he faced were not unique to Tarvel; they echoed in communities around the world, highlighting the universal nature of the fight for liberation.

In conclusion, Adin Xeris's emergence as the face of LGBTQ liberation was a multifaceted journey marked by personal growth, societal challenges, and collective action. His story serves as a reminder that representation matters, and that the fight for equality is a shared responsibility that requires courage, resilience, and unwavering commitment. As Adin continued to advocate for change, he not only transformed his own life but also ignited a movement that would resonate for generations to come.

Speaking at national LGBTQ conferences

As Adin Xeris's reputation as an activist grew, so did the opportunities to address larger audiences at national LGBTQ conferences. These gatherings became pivotal platforms for Adin to amplify the voices of marginalized communities, advocate for policy changes, and share personal stories that resonated with many. The experience of speaking at these conferences was not only a significant milestone in Adin's activism but also a reflection of the broader struggles faced by the LGBTQ community.

The Importance of National Conferences

National LGBTQ conferences serve multiple purposes: they are arenas for networking, knowledge-sharing, and strategizing. Attendees come together from diverse backgrounds, united by a common cause—advocating for equality and justice. Adin's participation in these conferences exemplified the intersection of personal narrative and political action, a theme that resonated throughout the LGBTQ rights movement.

Theoretical frameworks such as *Critical Queer Theory* suggest that personal narratives can challenge dominant cultural narratives and foster a sense of community among marginalized individuals. Adin's speeches often drew upon this theory, emphasizing the importance of storytelling in activism. By sharing his journey, Adin not only humanized the statistics surrounding LGBTQ issues but also inspired others to share their stories, creating a ripple effect of empowerment.

Challenges Faced on the National Stage

However, speaking at national conferences was not without its challenges. Adin faced the pressure of representing not only himself but the entire LGBTQ community. The weight of expectations can be daunting, especially when addressing issues such as discrimination, violence, and the ongoing fight for legal rights. Adin often remarked, "When I step onto that stage, it's not just me talking; it's every kid in Tarvel who's afraid to be themselves."

One significant challenge was navigating the balance between personal vulnerability and the need for a strong, united front. Adin understood that while sharing personal experiences could foster connection, it also left him open to scrutiny and criticism. The fear of backlash from conservative factions, who often attended these conferences to disrupt or discredit LGBTQ voices, was ever-present.

Examples of Impactful Speeches

Adin's speeches at these conferences often included poignant anecdotes that illustrated the struggles faced by LGBTQ individuals in conservative areas like Tarvel. For instance, during the annual *Pride in Politics* conference, Adin recounted a harrowing experience of facing hostility during a local town hall meeting. He described how a simple question about LGBTQ rights turned into a barrage of hate-filled comments. This narrative not only highlighted the challenges of activism but also underscored the importance of resilience.

Another memorable moment occurred at the *National LGBTQ Advocacy Summit*, where Adin spoke about the significance of intersectionality in activism. He stated, "Our fight is not just for visibility; it's for the rights of every individual, regardless of their race, gender, or socioeconomic status." This statement resonated deeply with attendees, sparking discussions about the need for inclusive practices within the LGBTQ movement.

Adin's ability to weave personal stories with broader social issues made his speeches impactful. He often utilized rhetorical devices such as *anaphora* and *pathos* to engage his audience emotionally. For example, he would repeat phrases like "We deserve..." to emphasize the collective rights of the LGBTQ community, creating a powerful call to action.

The Aftermath of Speaking Engagements

The aftermath of Adin's speeches often resulted in increased media attention and public support for LGBTQ rights in Tarvel and beyond. Following his address at the *Annual LGBTQ Rights Conference*, several attendees reached out to Adin, expressing their desire to collaborate on local initiatives. This response illustrated the potential for national conferences to serve as catalysts for grassroots activism.

Adin also faced criticism and pushback from conservative groups following these speaking engagements. However, he remained undeterred, viewing opposition as a sign that his message was resonating. He famously quipped, "If they're not mad, I'm not doing it right!" This attitude not only showcased his resilience but also inspired other activists to stand firm in their convictions, regardless of the backlash they might face.

Conclusion

In conclusion, speaking at national LGBTQ conferences was a transformative experience for Adin Xeris. These platforms allowed him to share his story, advocate for change, and connect with a broader community of activists. Despite the challenges, Adin's ability to articulate the struggles and triumphs of the LGBTQ community resonated with many, solidifying his role as a leading voice in the fight for equality. The impact of his speeches extended beyond the conference walls, fostering a sense of solidarity and inspiring a new generation of activists to continue the fight for LGBTQ rights.

Through his journey, Adin demonstrated that the power of storytelling and the courage to speak out could indeed change hearts and minds, making a lasting impact on the ongoing struggle for justice and equality.

The controversies surrounding Adin

Adin Xeris was not only a beacon of hope for many in the LGBTQ community of Tarvel; he was also a lightning rod for controversy. As he rose to prominence as an activist, the media spotlight intensified, revealing the complexities and challenges that come with being a public figure advocating for change. This section explores the controversies that surrounded Adin, examining the dynamics of public perception, media representation, and the backlash from conservative factions.

Media Representation and Misinterpretations

One of the primary sources of controversy for Adin stemmed from how the media portrayed him. While many outlets celebrated his activism, others were quick to sensationalize his story, often misrepresenting his intentions and actions. For instance, during the coverage of the first LGBTQ Awareness March in Tarvel, headlines ranged from "Local Hero Leads the Charge for Equality" to "Radical Activist Sparks Uproar." This duality in representation can be understood through the lens of *Framing Theory*, which posits that the way information is presented can significantly influence public perception [?].

The framing of Adin as both a hero and a radical created a polarized environment. Supporters rallied behind him, while detractors used the sensationalized narratives to galvanize opposition. For example, conservative groups utilized media misinterpretations to argue that Adin was promoting an agenda that threatened traditional family values. This led to heated debates in community forums and social media platforms, where Adin often found himself defending his position against a tide of misinformation.

Backlash from Conservative Groups

As Adin's visibility grew, so did the backlash from conservative factions in Tarvel. These groups, feeling threatened by the changes Adin advocated for, launched campaigns to undermine his credibility. One notable instance was a protest organized by a local conservative organization, which claimed that Adin's activism was a "corruption of youth." This protest was not merely a local issue; it drew national attention, leading to a polarized discussion on LGBTQ rights in the media.

The backlash can be analyzed through *Social Identity Theory*, which suggests that individuals derive part of their identity from the groups they belong to. For many conservatives in Tarvel, the rise of LGBTQ activism represented a challenge to their social identity and values. Consequently, they rallied against Adin, framing him as an outsider attempting to impose his views on a community that did not share his beliefs [?].

Controversial Statements and Actions

Adin's journey was also marked by controversial statements and actions that sparked debate within both the LGBTQ community and the broader public. One such incident occurred during a national LGBTQ conference, where Adin made a bold statement suggesting that "compromise is a betrayal of our community." While many applauded his passion, others criticized him for being divisive. This incident highlights the tension between radical and moderate approaches within activist movements.

The discourse surrounding this statement can be contextualized using *Critical Theory*, which emphasizes the importance of questioning societal norms and advocating for radical change. Adin's assertion challenged the status quo, but it also alienated some potential allies who believed in a more conciliatory approach to activism [?]. The internal conflict within the LGBTQ community became evident, as differing opinions on strategy led to factionalism, complicating the fight for equality.

The Impact of Social Media

In the age of social media, Adin's controversies were amplified exponentially. Platforms like Twitter and Instagram became battlegrounds where supporters and critics engaged in heated debates. Memes, hashtags, and viral videos often misrepresented Adin's message, leading to further polarization. For example, a viral video of Adin's speech at a protest was edited to make it appear as though he was inciting violence, which led to a wave of outrage and calls for his resignation from various advocacy positions.

This phenomenon can be understood through *Networked Publics Theory*, which posits that social media creates new forms of public discourse that can both empower and endanger activists [?]. While Adin used these platforms to mobilize support, he also faced the risk of being misrepresented in ways that could undermine his credibility and the cause he championed.

Navigating Controversy

Despite the controversies, Adin navigated these challenges with resilience and strategic acumen. He recognized the importance of addressing misinformation directly. Adin often engaged in public forums and social media discussions to clarify his positions and counteract false narratives. His approach exemplified the principle of *Crisis Communication*, which emphasizes proactive engagement and transparency as essential strategies for managing public perception during controversies [?].

Furthermore, Adin's ability to build coalitions with other activists and community leaders helped mitigate some of the backlash. By fostering dialogue between differing factions, he aimed to bridge divides and promote a more inclusive approach to advocacy. This strategy not only strengthened his position but also highlighted the importance of unity in the face of adversity.

Conclusion

In conclusion, the controversies surrounding Adin Xeris were multifaceted, reflecting the complexities of activism in a polarized society. Through media representation, backlash from conservative groups, and the challenges posed by social media, Adin's journey illustrates the delicate balance activists must strike between passion and pragmatism. Ultimately, these controversies shaped Adin's legacy, reinforcing the notion that the fight for LGBTQ rights is fraught with challenges but also ripe with opportunities for growth and change.

Meeting prominent LGBTQ activists

As Adin Xeris's journey into activism deepened, he found himself in the exhilarating yet daunting position of meeting some of the most influential LGBTQ activists of his time. These encounters were not just milestones in his career; they were transformative experiences that shaped his understanding of the movement and his role within it.

The Weight of Legacy

Meeting established activists like Marsha P. Johnson and Sylvia Rivera, both pivotal figures in the Stonewall uprising, was akin to standing in the shadow of giants. Adin learned that activism is not just about the present struggles but also about honoring the legacy of those who fought before him. He was struck by the stories of resilience and courage that defined their journeys. For instance, Johnson's famous declaration, "No pride for some of us without liberation for all of us," resonated deeply with Adin, reinforcing his belief in intersectionality within the movement.

The Power of Collaboration

Adin soon realized that activism thrives on collaboration. At a national LGBTQ conference, he had the opportunity to meet prominent figures like RuPaul and Laverne Cox. Their insights into the entertainment industry's role in shaping public perception of LGBTQ issues opened Adin's eyes to the power of visibility. RuPaul's mantra, "You better work!" became a personal motto for Adin, reminding him that activism, much like performance, requires authenticity and effort.

The Challenges of Recognition

However, these meetings were not without their challenges. Adin faced the harsh reality of competition within the activist community. Some prominent activists were wary of newcomers, fearing that their voices would be drowned out in the cacophony of emerging voices. This tension highlighted the ongoing struggle for recognition and representation within the LGBTQ movement. Adin learned that visibility does not guarantee acceptance; it must be earned through genuine commitment and collaboration.

Building Alliances

During these encounters, Adin also recognized the importance of building alliances beyond the LGBTQ community. Meeting with activists from various social justice movements, such as Black Lives Matter and the Women's March, helped him understand the interconnectedness of their struggles. He realized that LGBTQ rights are deeply intertwined with issues of race, gender, and economic inequality. This intersectional approach became a cornerstone of Adin's activism, as he began to advocate for a more inclusive movement that addressed the needs of all marginalized communities.

Mentorship and Guidance

One of the most significant impacts of meeting prominent activists was the mentorship he received. Figures like Janet Mock and Billy Porter took Adin under their wings, providing invaluable guidance on navigating the complexities of activism. They emphasized the importance of self-care and mental health, reminding him that even the fiercest warriors need to recharge. Adin learned that activism is a marathon, not a sprint, and that sustainability is key to long-term success.

Inspiration and Motivation

These meetings served as a source of inspiration for Adin. He began to incorporate the lessons learned from these activists into his own work. For example, he organized workshops focused on storytelling, drawing from the experiences of LGBTQ individuals in Tarvel. Adin believed that sharing personal narratives was a powerful tool for fostering empathy and understanding in a community often plagued by ignorance and prejudice.

The Ripple Effect

As Adin continued to meet and collaborate with prominent activists, he noticed a ripple effect in his own community. Their encouragement and support emboldened him to take bold actions, such as organizing the first LGBTQ Awareness March in Tarvel. The presence of well-known activists lent credibility to his efforts, attracting media attention and galvanizing local support.

In conclusion, meeting prominent LGBTQ activists was a pivotal moment in Adin Xeris's journey. These encounters not only shaped his understanding of activism but also equipped him with the tools and inspiration needed to amplify his voice and the voices of those in his community. Adin emerged from these experiences with a renewed sense of purpose, ready to fight for equality and justice with the knowledge that he was part of a larger, interconnected movement.

The formation of Adin's advocacy group

In the burgeoning landscape of LGBTQ activism in Tarvel, Adin Xeris recognized the necessity of a structured organization to amplify the voices of the marginalized and create a sustainable platform for advocacy. The formation of Adin's advocacy group, which would come to be known as *Tarvel Equality Alliance (TEA)*, was not just a response to the pressing need for representation; it was a strategic move to harness the collective power of the community.

Theoretical Framework

The theoretical underpinning of Adin's advocacy group can be traced back to the *Collective Action Theory*. This theory posits that individuals are more likely to engage in activism when they perceive that collective efforts can lead to significant social change. According to [1], individuals often face the dilemma of free-riding when participating in collective action, as the benefits of activism are shared among all members, regardless of individual contribution. Adin aimed to counteract this tendency by fostering a sense of belonging and shared purpose within the group.

Identifying Problems

Before the establishment of TEA, the LGBTQ community in Tarvel faced several critical issues:

- **Lack of Representation:** Local governance was predominantly conservative, leading to policies that marginalized LGBTQ voices. Adin identified that without a unified front, the community would continue to be ignored.

- **Safety Concerns:** Many individuals were afraid to express their identities openly due to threats of violence and discrimination. The group aimed to create a safe space for dialogue and support.

- **Limited Resources:** Activists were often isolated, lacking access to resources necessary for effective campaigning. TEA sought to pool resources and knowledge to empower members.

Formation Process

The formation of TEA involved several key steps, which can be summarized as follows:

Step 1: Community Engagement   Adin organized community meetings to gauge interest and gather input from potential members. These meetings served as a platform for individuals to share their experiences and articulate their needs. Adin employed techniques from *Participatory Action Research* to ensure that the voices of the community were central to the group's mission.

Step 2: Establishing a Mission Statement   With input from community members, TEA developed a mission statement that emphasized inclusivity, advocacy for legal rights, and the promotion of mental health awareness within the LGBTQ community. The mission statement read:

> "The Tarvel Equality Alliance is dedicated to fostering a safe and inclusive environment for all LGBTQ individuals, advocating for equal rights, and supporting mental health initiatives within our community."

Step 3: Structuring the Organization   Adin and a core group of volunteers established a leadership structure that included roles such as President, Vice President, Secretary, and Treasurer. This structure was designed to distribute responsibilities evenly and encourage participation from all members. According to [2], a well-defined organizational structure is crucial for effective governance and accountability.

Step 4: Fundraising and Resource Allocation   Recognizing the need for financial sustainability, TEA initiated fundraising campaigns, including local events, online crowdfunding, and partnerships with sympathetic businesses. The group allocated funds towards educational programs, community outreach, and legal advocacy efforts.

Examples of Early Initiatives

The initial activities of TEA reflected its mission and commitment to advocacy:

+ **Support Groups:** TEA launched weekly support groups for LGBTQ individuals, providing a safe space to discuss personal challenges and share resources.

+ **Awareness Campaigns:** The group organized awareness campaigns during Pride Month, utilizing social media platforms to educate the wider community about LGBTQ issues and rights.

+ **Legal Workshops:** TEA hosted workshops led by legal experts to educate members about their rights and the legal processes surrounding discrimination and harassment.

Challenges Faced

Despite the initial enthusiasm, TEA encountered several challenges:

+ **Resistance from Conservative Groups:** The formation of TEA was met with backlash from conservative factions in Tarvel, who viewed the group as a threat to traditional values. This resistance highlighted the ongoing cultural battle surrounding LGBTQ rights.

+ **Internal Conflicts:** As with any grassroots organization, differing opinions and priorities led to internal conflicts. Adin emphasized the importance of open communication and conflict resolution strategies, drawing from *Transformative Leadership Theory* to navigate these challenges.

+ **Resource Limitations:** Securing consistent funding remained a struggle, limiting the group's ability to expand its initiatives. Adin sought to address this by diversifying funding sources and applying for grants aimed at supporting LGBTQ organizations.

Conclusion

The formation of the Tarvel Equality Alliance marked a significant turning point in the LGBTQ movement within Tarvel. Under Adin's leadership, the group not only provided a platform for advocacy but also fostered a sense of community and empowerment among its members. As TEA continued to grow and evolve, it became a beacon of hope and resilience, demonstrating the power of collective action in the face of adversity. The legacy of this organization would resonate far beyond the borders of Tarvel, inspiring similar movements across the country.

Bibliography

[1] M. Olson, *The Logic of Collective Action: Public Goods and the Theory of Groups*, Harvard University Press, 1965.

[2] H. Mintzberg, *The Structuring of Organizations: A Synthesis of the Research*, Prentice Hall, 1979.

Fighting for Legal Rights

Lobbying for LGBTQ anti-discrimination laws

In the heart of the battle for LGBTQ rights, lobbying for anti-discrimination laws emerged as a pivotal strategy for activists like Adin Xeris. This section explores the theoretical underpinnings of lobbying, the problems faced by advocates, and real-world examples that illustrate both the challenges and successes of these efforts.

Theoretical Framework of Lobbying

Lobbying, at its core, is the act of influencing decisions made by government officials, typically legislators or members of regulatory agencies. The theory behind lobbying is grounded in the concept of pluralism, which posits that a multitude of groups compete to influence public policy. According to [?], effective lobbying is characterized by several key elements:

- **Access to Decision-Makers:** Successful lobbying requires establishing connections with lawmakers who can influence legislation.

- **Strategic Messaging:** Crafting clear and persuasive messages that resonate with both lawmakers and the public is crucial.

✦ **Coalition Building:** Forming alliances with other advocacy groups can amplify the impact of lobbying efforts.

Challenges in Lobbying for LGBTQ Rights

Despite the theoretical advantages, LGBTQ activists faced significant challenges in their lobbying efforts:

✦ **Hostile Political Climate:** In many regions, conservative values dominated the political landscape, making it difficult to gain traction for LGBTQ anti-discrimination laws. For instance, in Tarvel, the local government was resistant to any form of legislation perceived as promoting LGBTQ rights.

✦ **Misinformation and Stigma:** Misinformation about LGBTQ individuals often fueled prejudice, complicating the task of advocates. Adin's team frequently encountered opposition based on stereotypes and unfounded fears regarding the LGBTQ community.

✦ **Limited Resources:** Many LGBTQ advocacy groups operated on shoestring budgets, limiting their ability to conduct extensive lobbying campaigns. This financial constraint often hindered their capacity to reach lawmakers effectively.

Strategies Employed by Adin and Allies

Adin Xeris and his allies employed several strategies to navigate these challenges:

✦ **Grassroots Mobilization:** Adin understood that mobilizing community support was essential. He organized town hall meetings and community forums to educate the public about LGBTQ rights, fostering a groundswell of support that could not be ignored by lawmakers.

✦ **Utilizing Social Media:** In the digital age, social media became a powerful tool for advocacy. Adin's team leveraged platforms like Twitter and Instagram to spread awareness and rally support. Hashtags such as #TarvelForEquality trended locally, bringing attention to their cause.

✦ **Direct Engagement with Legislators:** Adin and his team scheduled meetings with local representatives, presenting compelling data and personal stories to illustrate the need for anti-discrimination laws. For example, they shared statistics showing that LGBTQ individuals were disproportionately affected by workplace discrimination, using the following equation to highlight the disparity:

$$D = \frac{N_{LGBTQ}}{N_{Total}} \times 100 \qquad (27)$$

Where D represents the discrimination rate, N_{LGBTQ} is the number of reported discrimination cases involving LGBTQ individuals, and N_{Total} is the total number of reported discrimination cases. This data-driven approach made it harder for lawmakers to dismiss their concerns.

Case Studies of Successful Lobbying Efforts

Several key victories in LGBTQ lobbying efforts serve as testament to the power of organized advocacy:

+ **The Equality Act of 2021:** While this federal legislation faced significant hurdles, it was a product of years of lobbying by LGBTQ advocates. The act aimed to expand the Civil Rights Act to include sexual orientation and gender identity, showcasing the importance of persistent advocacy.

+ **Local Wins in Tarvel:** Adin's efforts culminated in the passage of a local anti-discrimination ordinance in Tarvel, which prohibited discrimination based on sexual orientation and gender identity in employment, housing, and public accommodations. This victory was celebrated as a monumental step forward for the LGBTQ community in a historically conservative area.

Conclusion

Lobbying for LGBTQ anti-discrimination laws is a complex and often arduous process fraught with challenges. However, through strategic engagement, grassroots mobilization, and persistent advocacy, activists like Adin Xeris have made significant strides in the fight for equality. The lessons learned from these lobbying efforts continue to inform the ongoing struggle for LGBTQ rights, underscoring the necessity of resilience and community support in the face of adversity.

Challenging Tarvel's Marriage Equality Ban

The fight for marriage equality in Tarvel was not just a legal battle; it was a cultural revolution. Adin Xeris, now a prominent figure in the LGBTQ community, understood that the ban on same-sex marriage was a direct affront to the dignity and rights of countless individuals. The challenge was not merely to overturn a law but to shift the very fabric of societal beliefs deeply rooted in conservative values.

The Legal Framework

In Tarvel, the ban on same-sex marriage was codified in law, reflecting the views of a significant portion of the population. The legal arguments against this ban often centered around the principles of equality and non-discrimination enshrined in constitutional law. The following equation encapsulates the fundamental legal principle at stake:

$$E = \frac{(R_a + R_b)}{2} \to R_{eq} \tag{28}$$

Where: - E is the equality status, - R_a is the rights afforded to heterosexual couples, - R_b is the rights denied to same-sex couples, - R_{eq} is the resultant rights when equality is achieved.

This equation illustrates that true equality can only be achieved when the rights of all individuals are equal, irrespective of their sexual orientation.

Mobilizing the Community

Adin initiated a grassroots campaign to challenge the marriage equality ban. This involved organizing town hall meetings, rallies, and workshops that educated the community about the implications of the ban. The strategy was to use personal stories to humanize the issue, making it relatable to those who might not have understood the struggles faced by the LGBTQ community.

For instance, during one of the town hall meetings, Adin shared the story of two local women, Sarah and Emily, who had been together for over a decade but were denied the legal recognition of their relationship. Their story resonated with many attendees, some of whom had initially been indifferent to the issue. This emotional appeal was crucial in shifting public opinion.

Facing Opposition

The campaign was not without its challenges. Conservative groups, often backed by religious organizations, mounted a fierce opposition. They argued that marriage should be defined as a union between one man and one woman, invoking traditional values and religious beliefs. Adin faced threats, harassment, and even attempts to discredit his character.

In response, Adin and his supporters utilized social media as a platform to counter misinformation. They launched a campaign titled "#LoveIsLove," which aimed to promote positive narratives around same-sex relationships. The campaign included videos, testimonials, and statistics that highlighted the benefits of marriage equality, such as improved mental health outcomes for LGBTQ individuals.

Legal Actions and Court Challenges

Recognizing that public opinion alone would not suffice, Adin and his team of lawyers prepared to challenge the marriage ban in court. They filed a lawsuit arguing that the ban violated the Equal Protection Clause of the Tarvel Constitution. The legal strategy was grounded in the precedent set by other jurisdictions that had successfully overturned similar bans.

The legal team presented evidence showing that states with marriage equality experienced lower rates of mental health issues among LGBTQ citizens, arguing that the ban had direct harmful effects on the community's well-being. This data was critical in demonstrating that the ban was not just a legal issue but a public health concern.

The Landmark Court Case

The case, Xeris v. State of Tarvel, became a landmark moment in the fight for marriage equality. Adin took the stand, passionately articulating the need for equality and love. The courtroom was filled with supporters, and the media coverage was extensive, bringing national attention to Tarvel's struggle.

The judge's ruling was a pivotal moment: the court declared the marriage equality ban unconstitutional, citing that it violated the fundamental rights of individuals to marry whom they choose. The ruling was met with jubilation from supporters and was a significant victory for the LGBTQ community in Tarvel.

Celebrating the Victory

Following the court's decision, Adin organized a massive celebration in the town square. It was a moment of triumph, not just for the LGBTQ community but for all who believed in equality. The event featured speeches from local leaders, performances from LGBTQ artists, and a wedding ceremony for couples who had been waiting for this moment for years.

This victory in Tarvel served as an inspiration for other regions still grappling with marriage equality issues. Adin's determination and resilience became a beacon of hope, proving that love could indeed conquer all.

In conclusion, challenging Tarvel's marriage equality ban was a multifaceted battle that combined legal action, community mobilization, and personal storytelling. Adin Xeris emerged as a leader not just in Tarvel but as a symbol of the ongoing struggle for LGBTQ rights everywhere. The fight for equality was far from over, but this victory marked a significant step forward in the journey toward justice and acceptance.

Facing Backlash and Threats

In the tumultuous landscape of LGBTQ activism, facing backlash and threats is an unfortunate yet common reality. For Adin Xeris, the emergence as a leading activist in Tarvel was met with both fervent support and vehement opposition. This section delves into the nature of the backlash Adin faced, the theoretical frameworks that help us understand such phenomena, and the psychological and social implications of these threats.

The Nature of Backlash

Backlash against LGBTQ activists often manifests in various forms, including verbal harassment, social ostracism, and even physical threats. Adin's advocacy for LGBTQ rights in a conservative town like Tarvel was particularly polarizing. The local conservative groups, threatened by the changing tides of social acceptance, mobilized against Adin's initiatives.

One notable incident occurred during the planning of the first LGBTQ Awareness March in Tarvel. As the event gained traction, a local conservative organization distributed flyers that contained inflammatory language aimed at discrediting Adin and the LGBTQ community. The flyers claimed that the march would "corrupt the youth" and "destroy family values," a classic example of fear-based rhetoric often employed in backlash scenarios.

Theoretical Frameworks

To understand the backlash against LGBTQ activism, we can employ several sociological theories. One relevant framework is the *Social Identity Theory*, which posits that individuals derive a sense of identity from their group memberships. When Adin began to challenge the status quo, it threatened the identity of those who aligned with conservative values. This threat often leads to defensive reactions from the dominant group, resulting in backlash.

Additionally, the *Framing Theory* provides insight into how events and movements are perceived by the public. Adin's activism was framed by opponents as a threat to societal norms, which helped galvanize conservative forces against him. By labeling the LGBTQ movement as "radical" or "immoral," opponents aimed to rally support and legitimize their backlash.

Psychological Implications

The psychological effects of facing backlash can be profound. Adin experienced increased anxiety and stress as threats escalated. The constant fear of harassment not only affected his mental well-being but also his ability to engage in activism fully. Research indicates that activists facing backlash often experience symptoms of *vicarious trauma*, where the stress of potential violence or harassment impacts their mental health even if they haven't directly experienced it.

Moreover, the phenomenon of *imposter syndrome* can emerge in activists facing backlash. Adin, despite his growing recognition, often questioned his legitimacy as an activist, wondering if he was worthy of the title given the intense scrutiny and threats he faced. This internal conflict can hinder an activist's effectiveness and willingness to engage with their cause.

Real-Life Examples

Adin's experience was not unique. Many activists have faced similar threats. For instance, during the marriage equality debates in the United States, activists like Jim Obergefell received threats and harassment for their roles in advocating for legal recognition of same-sex marriage. Such threats are often amplified by social media, where anonymity can embolden aggressors to express hateful sentiments without fear of repercussions.

In Tarvel, Adin's advocacy group organized a rally in response to the backlash, using the opportunity to educate the community about LGBTQ issues. This counteraction was crucial, not only for raising awareness but also for reinforcing the community's resilience against hate. Adin's rally drew attention from local media, which further highlighted the importance of solidarity in the face of adversity.

Conclusion

Facing backlash and threats is an inevitable aspect of LGBTQ activism, particularly in conservative environments like Tarvel. Understanding the nature of this backlash through theoretical frameworks such as Social Identity Theory and Framing Theory provides valuable insights into the dynamics at play. The psychological implications of these threats can be debilitating, yet they also serve as a catalyst for resilience and community solidarity.

Adin Xeris's experience exemplifies the courage required to stand against such adversity, illustrating that while the path of activism is fraught with challenges, it is also paved with opportunities for growth, understanding, and ultimately, change. The fight for LGBTQ rights is not merely a personal struggle; it is a collective journey that demands strength in the face of opposition.

In the words of Adin himself, "If you're not facing backlash, you're probably not doing it right." This statement encapsulates the essence of activism: it is a bold declaration of identity and rights, and with that declaration often comes resistance. However, it is through this resistance that communities can rally, educate, and ultimately transform societal norms for the better.

The landmark Supreme Court case for LGBTQ rights

In the annals of LGBTQ history, few events resonate with the same magnitude as the landmark Supreme Court case that forever altered the legal landscape for queer individuals in Tarvel and beyond. This case, known as *Xeris v. Tarvel State*, emerged from a series of legal battles that highlighted the systemic discrimination faced by LGBTQ individuals, ultimately culminating in a ruling that would set a precedent for future rights and protections.

Background and Context

The roots of *Xeris v. Tarvel State* can be traced back to the oppressive environment in which Adin Xeris and many others lived. Tarvel, a town steeped in conservative values, had long upheld laws that not only discriminated against LGBTQ individuals but actively suppressed their rights to love, marry, and live freely. The case arose when Adin, alongside a coalition of activists, challenged the state's marriage equality ban, which was emblematic of a broader societal issue—discrimination based on sexual orientation.

Legal Framework

To understand the significance of the case, we must first examine the legal framework surrounding LGBTQ rights. Prior to *Xeris v. Tarvel State*, the legal landscape was characterized by a patchwork of state laws, with some states recognizing same-sex marriage while others imposed strict bans. The legal theory underpinning the case revolved around the Equal Protection Clause of the Fourteenth Amendment, which asserts that no state shall deny to any person within its jurisdiction the equal protection of the laws.

Equal Protection: $\forall x \in$ citizens, if x is treated differently based on y (where y is a protect

$$(29)$$

The Case Unfolds

As the case progressed, Adin and his legal team faced numerous challenges, including pushback from conservative groups who argued that the traditional definition of marriage should remain intact. The opposition relied heavily on historical precedents that favored heteronormative unions, asserting that any deviation from this norm would lead to societal decay.

Despite the daunting obstacles, Adin's team presented a robust argument that highlighted the psychological and social ramifications of discrimination. They showcased testimonies from individuals who had suffered due to the lack of legal recognition for their relationships, effectively humanizing the abstract legal arguments.

Key Arguments and Theories

Central to the case were several key arguments that would ultimately sway the court's decision:

+ **The Right to Love:** At the heart of the case was the assertion that love is a fundamental human right that transcends gender and sexual orientation. The plaintiffs argued that the state's refusal to recognize same-sex marriages was a violation of their personal freedoms.

+ **Social Stability:** The defense of marriage as a union between a man and a woman was countered with evidence showing that same-sex couples contribute positively to social stability, raising children and participating in community life just as heterosexual couples do.

♦ **Economic Discrimination:** The economic implications of denying marriage rights were also emphasized. The plaintiffs presented data illustrating how same-sex couples faced financial disadvantages, from tax penalties to lack of health benefits, which further entrenched economic inequality.

The Supreme Court Ruling

After months of deliberation, the Supreme Court delivered its ruling. In a landmark decision, the court ruled in favor of Adin Xeris and the plaintiffs, declaring that the state's marriage equality ban was unconstitutional. The majority opinion, authored by Justice Harris, stated:

> "The fundamental right to marry is inherent in the liberty of the person, and under the Equal Protection Clause, same-sex couples cannot be denied that right. To deny them this right is to deny them their dignity and their humanity."

This ruling was monumental, not only for the individuals involved but for the LGBTQ community as a whole. It signaled a shift in societal attitudes and laid the groundwork for future legal battles, reinforcing the notion that love knows no bounds.

Repercussions and Impact

The impact of *Xeris v. Tarvel State* reverberated throughout the nation. Following the ruling, several states that had previously upheld similar bans began to reconsider their stances. The case became a touchstone for LGBTQ rights activists, serving as a rallying cry for further advancements in equality.

Adin's advocacy group capitalized on this momentum, organizing educational campaigns and outreach programs to inform the public about the significance of the ruling. The case not only changed the legal landscape but also inspired a new generation of activists to continue the fight for equality.

Conclusion

In retrospect, *Xeris v. Tarvel State* was more than just a legal battle; it was a cultural revolution. It illustrated the power of grassroots activism and the importance of fighting for one's rights. Adin Xeris emerged not just as a legal figure but as a symbol of resilience and hope for countless individuals who dared to dream of a world where love is celebrated in all its forms.

This landmark case serves as a reminder that the fight for LGBTQ rights is ongoing, and while significant progress has been made, the principles of equality and justice must be vigilantly upheld.

Celebrating the victory of LGBTQ rights in Tarvel

The culmination of Adin Xeris's tireless efforts and the collective struggle of the LGBTQ community in Tarvel reached a monumental milestone: the official recognition of LGBTQ rights within the local legal framework. This victory was not merely a legal triumph; it symbolized a profound shift in societal attitudes and an affirmation of identity for countless individuals who had long been marginalized.

The Atmosphere of Celebration

On the day of the announcement, the atmosphere in Tarvel was electric. The news spread like wildfire, igniting spontaneous celebrations across the city. Rainbow flags waved proudly from windows, and the streets were filled with jubilant crowds chanting slogans of love and equality. This moment marked a departure from the shadows of fear and repression, allowing the community to bask in the warmth of acceptance.

> "Today, we stand not just as individuals, but as a united front against discrimination!" shouted Adin from the steps of the town hall, the crowd erupting in applause.

Theoretical Framework: Social Change and Collective Identity

To understand the significance of this victory, we can apply social movement theory, particularly the concept of collective identity as posited by Polletta and Jasper (2001). Collective identity refers to the shared sense of belonging and purpose among members of a social group. In the case of Tarvel, the LGBTQ community's collective identity was forged through years of struggle, resilience, and solidarity.

The successful push for legal rights can be articulated through the following equation:

$$\text{Legal Recognition} = f(\text{Collective Identity, Activism, Public Support}) \quad (30)$$

where: - Legal Recognition denotes the formal acknowledgment of LGBTQ rights, - Collective Identity reflects the unity and shared experiences of the community, - Activism encompasses the organized efforts to advocate for rights, and - Public Support indicates the broader societal backing that legitimizes these efforts.

Challenges Faced and Overcome

However, this victory did not come without its challenges. The road to legal recognition was fraught with opposition from conservative factions within Tarvel. These groups employed various tactics to undermine the movement, from misinformation campaigns to organized protests. For instance, during the lead-up to the legal vote, a local conservative organization launched a campaign filled with fear-mongering rhetoric, claiming that LGBTQ rights would lead to the erosion of traditional family values.

Adin and fellow activists countered this narrative through strategic outreach and education. They organized community forums where residents could engage in dialogue, dispelling myths and fostering understanding. This grassroots approach was instrumental in swaying public opinion.

The Role of Media and Public Engagement

The media played a pivotal role in shaping the narrative around LGBTQ rights in Tarvel. Local news outlets began to cover the movement more positively, showcasing stories of individuals who had faced discrimination and highlighting the benefits of inclusivity. Adin's charisma and eloquence made him a media darling, often appearing on talk shows and news segments to advocate for equality.

A significant turning point came when a documentary crew followed Adin and his advocacy group during the months leading up to the legal vote. The film, titled *Voices of Tarvel*, captured the raw emotions and struggles of the community, humanizing the fight for rights. The documentary not only garnered national attention but also fostered empathy among viewers, further solidifying public support.

Celebratory Events and Community Solidarity

In the aftermath of the legal victory, the community organized a series of celebratory events, including a grand parade that would become an annual tradition in Tarvel. The first parade, aptly named *Tarvel Pride*, drew thousands of participants and spectators alike. It featured colorful floats, live music, and speeches from local leaders, including Adin, who reflected on the journey:

> "This is not just a victory for us; it is a victory for humanity! We have shown that love triumphs over hate!"

The parade served as a platform for LGBTQ individuals to share their stories, fostering a sense of pride and belonging. It also attracted allies from various backgrounds, reinforcing the idea that the fight for equality transcends sexual orientation.

Legacy and Future Implications

The victory in Tarvel set a precedent for other conservative regions grappling with similar issues. It demonstrated that change is possible through unity, resilience, and strategic activism. Adin's advocacy group began receiving inquiries from activists in neighboring towns, eager to replicate the success in their own communities.

In conclusion, the celebration of LGBTQ rights in Tarvel was not merely an end but a new beginning. It marked the dawn of a more inclusive society, where love and acceptance could flourish. The journey ahead was still fraught with challenges, but the victory was a testament to the power of collective action and the indomitable spirit of the LGBTQ community.

Adin's Personal Struggles

Adin's Personal Struggles

Adin's Personal Struggles

Adin Xeris, the face of LGBTQ activism in Tarvel, was not just battling external forces; he was wrestling with his own demons. You see, activism can be like trying to juggle flaming swords while riding a unicycle on a tightrope. The pressure is real, and the stakes are high. In this chapter, we delve into the personal struggles that shaped Adin into the fearless warrior he became.

Navigating Love and Relationships

In a world where love should be as easy as pie, Adin found himself in a dating scene that felt more like a pie-eating contest—messy, complicated, and filled with unexpected surprises. Picture this: Adin, fresh out of the closet, swiping right on dating apps with the enthusiasm of a kid in a candy store. But instead of sweet treats, he was met with a buffet of heartbreaks and awkward encounters.

Adin's first relationship was like a rom-com gone wrong. He met Jamie at an LGBTQ mixer, where the atmosphere was charged with hope, glitter, and just a hint of desperation. They hit it off, sharing stories about their struggles and dreams. But as their relationship blossomed, so did the pressures of public scrutiny. Adin found himself questioning if love could survive in the spotlight.

The heartbreak came swiftly when Jamie decided they needed "space." Adin was left sitting on his couch, binge-watching reality TV, and wondering if his love life was a never-ending episode of "Survivor." The emotional toll was heavy, and recovery felt like trying to climb Mount Everest with flip-flops on. Yet, through the pain, Adin learned valuable lessons about vulnerability and the importance of self-love.

Mental Health and Burnout

As Adin's activism gained momentum, so did the weight of expectations. Balancing the demands of being an activist and maintaining his mental health was akin to walking a tightrope while juggling flaming swords—one misstep, and it could all come crashing down. The pressure to be a role model, to always be "on," and to represent an entire community was overwhelming.

Adin found himself battling anxiety and depression, feelings that crept in like uninvited guests at a party. The constant barrage of negativity from conservative groups and the media took a toll on his mental well-being. It was during one particularly dark moment that Adin realized he needed help. He sought professional therapy, a decision that felt as liberating as coming out all over again.

In therapy, Adin discovered the power of mindfulness and self-care. He learned that taking a break wasn't a sign of weakness; it was a necessary step in preserving his strength. Just like a phone needs to be charged to function, so did Adin. He began prioritizing his mental health, sharing his journey with others, and inspiring them to do the same.

Family and Acceptance

Navigating family dynamics can be like walking through a minefield—one wrong step, and boom! Adin's relationship with his conservative family was no different. While they loved him, their beliefs often clashed with his identity. Adin struggled to reconcile their expectations with his truth, feeling like a contestant on a reality show where the prize was acceptance.

In a heartfelt conversation over a holiday dinner, Adin bravely opened up about his experiences as an LGBTQ individual. The room fell silent, forks suspended in mid-air. He spoke of love, acceptance, and the importance of being true to oneself. To his surprise, his family listened. They didn't fully understand, but they made an effort to bridge the gap.

Through this process, Adin discovered the beauty of chosen family—the supportive LGBTQ community that embraced him with open arms. They became his safe haven, a reminder that love transcends blood ties. Adin learned to honor the elders of the LGBTQ movement, recognizing their sacrifices and the path they paved for future generations.

In conclusion, Adin's personal struggles were not just obstacles; they were the crucible that forged his identity as an activist. Love, mental health, and family acceptance shaped his journey, reminding us all that even the fiercest warriors have battles to fight within. Adin Xeris emerged not only as a champion for LGBTQ rights but also as a beacon of hope for those navigating the complexities of life, love, and identity.

As we continue to follow Adin's journey, we see that the fight for equality is not just a public battle; it's a deeply personal one. And in the words of Adin himself, "If you can't love yourself, how in the hell you gonna love somebody else?" Remember, folks, self-love is the foundation of all love—so let's build that foundation strong!

Navigating Love and Relationships

Adin's experiences in the dating scene

Navigating the dating scene as an LGBTQ activist in the conservative town of Tarvel was akin to walking a tightrope over a pit of snapping crocodiles. Adin's experiences were not just about finding love; they were a reflection of the broader societal tensions that existed in a community where acceptance was often a privilege rather than a right.

The Initial Foray into Dating

Adin's journey into the dating world began with a mix of excitement and trepidation. As he stepped into the realm of online dating, he quickly learned that the virtual landscape was both liberating and fraught with challenges. The initial thrill of swiping right on potential matches was often overshadowed by the weight of societal expectations and the fear of rejection.

$$R = \frac{E}{C} \tag{31}$$

Where R is the rate of rejection, E is the emotional investment, and C is the courage required to put oneself out there. In Adin's case, the emotional investment was high, as he was not just seeking companionship but also affirmation of his identity in a world that often sought to invalidate it.

The Challenges of Authenticity

As Adin began to meet people, he faced the daunting task of being authentic in a space where many were still in the closet. He often found himself in conversations where he had to gauge the level of comfort and acceptance of his date. This led to a series of awkward moments, where jokes about being "too gay" or comments about stereotypes would surface, leaving Adin feeling like he was in a never-ending episode of a bad sitcom.

$$A = \sum_{i=1}^{n}(C_i \cdot D_i) \tag{32}$$

Where A represents Adin's overall dating satisfaction, C_i is the compatibility score of each date, and D_i is the discomfort factor associated with societal pressures. The struggle for authenticity often resulted in a low compatibility score, as many dates ended with Adin feeling more like an activist than a romantic partner.

Love in Unlikely Places

Despite these challenges, Adin's resilience shone through. He discovered that love often blossomed in the most unexpected places. One memorable date involved a local coffee shop that doubled as a safe haven for LGBTQ youth. There, amidst the aroma of freshly brewed coffee and the sound of laughter, Adin found a connection with someone who shared his passion for activism.

This experience highlighted a crucial aspect of LGBTQ dating: the importance of shared values. Adin realized that finding a partner who understood the nuances of his life as an activist made all the difference. It was not just about romantic attraction; it was about finding someone who could navigate the complexities of societal expectations alongside him.

The Role of Community Support

Adin's dating experiences were also shaped by the support of the LGBTQ community in Tarvel. Friends became confidants, providing advice and sometimes even acting as wingmen. They created a network of solidarity that allowed Adin to explore his romantic interests with a sense of security.

$$S = \frac{N}{D} \tag{33}$$

Where S is the support level, N is the number of supportive friends, and D is the degree of danger perceived in the dating scene. In Adin's case, as he built his community, the support level increased, allowing him to approach dating with a newfound confidence.

Heartbreak and Growth

However, not all experiences were positive. Adin faced heartbreak, not just from romantic relationships that fizzled out, but also from those who were unwilling to accept his identity. These experiences were painful, yet they contributed to his growth as both an individual and an activist. Adin learned that heartbreak was not a sign of failure but rather an opportunity to reflect on what he truly wanted in a partner.

The Intersection of Activism and Romance

Ultimately, Adin's dating experiences were deeply intertwined with his activism. Each relationship brought new insights into the challenges faced by the LGBTQ community. Adin became acutely aware of how societal pressures could infiltrate personal relationships, and he used these experiences to fuel his advocacy work.

In conclusion, Adin's journey through the dating scene was a microcosm of the larger struggle for LGBTQ acceptance. It was filled with moments of joy, heartbreak, and invaluable lessons about love, identity, and community. As he continued to navigate this complex landscape, Adin emerged not only as a passionate activist but also as a person who understood the profound impact of love and connection in the fight for equality.

Heartbreak and Recovery

Heartbreak is a universal experience, a rite of passage that transcends age, culture, and sexual orientation. For Adin Xeris, navigating the turbulent waters of love in the public eye was akin to walking a tightrope—one misstep, and the fall could be catastrophic. This subsection delves into the emotional turmoil of heartbreak and the arduous journey towards recovery, exploring both personal anecdotes and broader psychological theories that illuminate this complex process.

The Weight of Expectations

In the realm of LGBTQ activism, where visibility often equates to vulnerability, Adin felt the pressure of expectations from both the community and society at large. The belief that as an activist, he should embody resilience and strength created a paradox: how could he advocate for love and acceptance while grappling with his own heartache? This tension often left him feeling isolated, as though he were trapped in a glass box—visible to all yet unable to connect meaningfully with anyone.

$$E = mc^2 \tag{34}$$

Where E represents emotional energy, m symbolizes the mass of expectations, and c is the speed of societal judgment. This equation humorously underscores the weight of societal pressures that can amplify the pain of heartbreak.

The Stages of Heartbreak

Psychologists often refer to the stages of grief, which can be applied to the experience of heartbreak. These stages include denial, anger, bargaining, depression, and acceptance. Adin's journey through these stages was tumultuous, often overlapping and spiraling into a cyclical pattern that left him emotionally drained.

+ **Denial:** Initially, Adin dismissed the reality of his heartbreak, convincing himself that everything was fine. He maintained a façade of confidence, often posting inspirational quotes on social media, masking his internal struggle.

+ **Anger:** As the truth began to seep in, anger took root. Adin found himself lashing out at friends and allies, projecting his pain onto those who cared for him. This phase was marked by a series of confrontations that left him feeling even more isolated.

+ **Bargaining:** In this stage, Adin attempted to negotiate with his emotions. He reached out to his ex, hoping to rekindle the flame, believing that if he could just fix the past, his heart would heal.

+ **Depression:** Eventually, the weight of his heartbreak became unbearable. Adin sank into a deep depression, characterized by sleepless nights and a loss of motivation. The once vibrant activist found it challenging to muster the energy to engage in the very movements he had championed.

+ **Acceptance:** After much introspection and support from his chosen family within the LGBTQ community, Adin began to accept his heartbreak as part of his journey. This acceptance did not signify the end of his pain, but rather a recognition that healing was possible.

The Role of Community Support

During his darkest days, Adin discovered the profound impact of community support. Friends and fellow activists rallied around him, reminding him that heartbreak, while deeply personal, is also a shared experience. This collective understanding fostered a sense of belonging that was crucial for his recovery.

> "The greatest gift of community is the reminder that you are not alone in your struggles."

Adin's experience echoes the theory of social support, which posits that individuals with strong social networks tend to recover more quickly from emotional distress. Research indicates that social support can mitigate the effects of stress and promote resilience during challenging times (Cohen & Wills, 1985).

The Path to Recovery

Recovery from heartbreak is not linear; it is a process that requires patience and self-compassion. Adin's path to healing involved several key strategies:

1. **Self-Care:** Adin prioritized self-care, engaging in activities that brought him joy, such as painting and hiking. These outlets provided a healthy distraction and allowed him to reconnect with himself.

2. **Therapy:** Seeking professional help was a pivotal step in Adin's recovery. Therapy provided a safe space for him to unpack his feelings and develop coping strategies.

3. **Creative Expression:** Adin turned to writing as a means of processing his emotions. He penned heartfelt letters to his past self, exploring the lessons learned from his heartbreak.

4. **Advocacy as Healing:** Channeling his pain into activism became a source of empowerment. Adin organized workshops focused on emotional health within the LGBTQ community, transforming his heartbreak into a catalyst for change.

Conclusion

Heartbreak is an inevitable part of the human experience, especially for those navigating the complexities of love within the LGBTQ community. For Adin

Xeris, the journey through heartbreak was fraught with challenges, yet it ultimately paved the way for personal growth and resilience. By embracing vulnerability and leaning on the support of his community, Adin not only healed but emerged stronger, ready to continue the fight for love and acceptance for all.

As Adin often reminded himself, "Heartbreak is not the end; it is merely a chapter in the story of love."

Bibliography

[1] Cohen, S., & Wills, T. A. (1985). Stress, social support, and the buffering hypothesis. *Psychological Bulletin*, 98(2), 310-357.

Sustaining a relationship in the public eye

In the realm of activism, where every action is scrutinized and every word is dissected, sustaining a relationship in the public eye presents unique challenges and opportunities. For Adin Xeris, navigating love while being a prominent LGBTQ activist was akin to walking a tightrope strung between two skyscrapers—one side representing the fervor of public support, the other, the weight of public opinion.

Theoretical Framework

The dynamics of public relationships can be examined through the lens of social identity theory, which posits that individuals derive a part of their self-concept from their perceived membership in social groups. In Adin's case, the intersection of his identity as an LGBTQ activist and as a partner in a romantic relationship created a complex interplay of personal and public personas. The theory suggests that when individuals are in the public eye, their relationships may be subject to greater scrutiny, leading to heightened stress and anxiety (Tajfel & Turner, 1979).

Challenges Faced

One of the most significant challenges Adin faced was the constant media attention that accompanied his activism. The relationship became a subject of public discourse, where every romantic gesture could be interpreted as a political statement. This phenomenon is known as the *public-private dichotomy*, where the lines between personal life and public persona blur.

For instance, when Adin and his partner decided to attend a high-profile LGBTQ gala together, the media coverage was overwhelming. Headlines ranged from supportive to disparaging, with some outlets questioning the authenticity of their relationship. This scrutiny often led to feelings of inadequacy and pressure to perform, as if their love had to be a symbol of the movement rather than a genuine connection.

Balancing Act

To sustain their relationship, Adin and his partner developed a set of strategies to maintain their bond amidst the chaos. One effective approach was establishing boundaries regarding public appearances. They agreed on certain events where they would present themselves as a couple and others where they would attend separately. This allowed them to enjoy moments of intimacy away from the prying eyes of the public.

Moreover, they prioritized communication. Adin often expressed that the key to their relationship was discussing how they felt about public perceptions and media portrayals. This open dialogue fostered a sense of security, enabling both partners to feel validated in their experiences.

Examples of Resilience

Adin's relationship was tested during a particularly challenging time when a scandal erupted involving a misquote from a media outlet. The quote suggested that Adin's partner was not supportive of his activism, which ignited a firestorm on social media. Instead of succumbing to the pressure, Adin and his partner chose to address the issue head-on. They hosted a joint press conference, where they spoke candidly about their relationship, the challenges they faced, and their unwavering support for one another.

This act of transparency not only strengthened their bond but also resonated with their supporters, who appreciated their authenticity. It became a moment of resilience, showcasing that love could withstand external pressures and emerge stronger.

The Role of Community

Another vital aspect of sustaining their relationship was the support of the LGBTQ community. Adin and his partner found solace in their friends and allies, who provided a safe space to discuss their experiences. The community served as a buffer against the negativity they sometimes encountered, reminding them that their love was valid and worthy of celebration.

Adin often participated in community events where he would speak about the importance of love and support within the LGBTQ community. He emphasized that relationships should not only be about personal fulfillment but also about contributing to the larger narrative of acceptance and equality.

Conclusion

Sustaining a relationship in the public eye, particularly as an LGBTQ activist, is fraught with challenges that can test the strength of any partnership. Through the application of social identity theory, we can understand the complexities involved in maintaining a balance between personal and public life. Adin's journey illustrates that with effective communication, established boundaries, and a supportive community, it is possible to navigate the tumultuous waters of public scrutiny while nurturing a loving relationship. Ultimately, Adin and his partner's story is a testament to the power of love in the face of adversity, reminding us all that personal connections can thrive even under the spotlight.

Mental Health and Burnout

The challenges of balancing activism and self-care

In the vibrant yet tumultuous world of activism, the line between fighting for a cause and taking care of oneself often becomes blurred. For Adin Xeris, as he emerged as a leading voice in the LGBTQ movement in Tarvel, this challenge became increasingly pronounced. The relentless push for equality and justice often left little room for personal well-being, leading to a complex interplay of passion, burnout, and the need for self-care.

Theoretical Framework

To understand the challenges Adin faced, we can draw upon the concept of *compassion fatigue*, which describes the emotional strain that activists and caregivers experience when they are constantly exposed to the suffering of others. According to Figley (1995), compassion fatigue can lead to symptoms akin to post-traumatic stress disorder, where the caregiver becomes overwhelmed by the emotional toll of their work. This theory provides a lens through which we can view Adin's struggles as he fought for LGBTQ rights while grappling with his own mental health.

The Problem of Burnout

As Adin became more involved in activism, he quickly found himself at the epicenter of numerous campaigns, rallies, and discussions. The pressure to be a constant source of inspiration and leadership often left him exhausted. Research by Maslach and Leiter (2016) identifies three key components of burnout: emotional exhaustion, depersonalization, and reduced personal accomplishment. Adin experienced all three as he poured his heart into the movement, feeling increasingly drained and detached from the very community he sought to uplift.

$$\text{Burnout} = f(E, D, PA)$$

where E represents emotional exhaustion, D is depersonalization, and PA signifies reduced personal accomplishment. As each factor increased, Adin's overall well-being diminished, leading to a cycle that threatened both his activism and his mental health.

Examples of Struggle

One poignant example of Adin's struggle with self-care occurred during the planning of the first LGBTQ Awareness March in Tarvel. As the date approached, the weight of expectations bore down on him. He found himself working late into the night, coordinating logistics, rallying support, and addressing media inquiries. Despite the excitement surrounding the event, Adin began to neglect his own needs—skipping meals, losing sleep, and isolating himself from friends and family.

Adin's friend and fellow activist, Maya, noticed his decline and urged him to take a step back. "You can't pour from an empty cup, Adin," she reminded him, echoing a popular adage that emphasizes the importance of self-care in sustaining one's capacity to help others. However, the guilt of taking time for himself weighed heavily on Adin. He felt that every moment spent away from activism was a moment lost in the fight for equality.

Strategies for Balance

Recognizing the need for balance, Adin began to explore various self-care strategies. He turned to mindfulness practices, such as meditation and yoga, which helped him reconnect with his body and mind. Research by Goyal et al. (2014) indicates that mindfulness can significantly reduce stress and improve emotional regulation, allowing individuals to better cope with the demands of their work.

$$\text{Mindfulness Impact} = \frac{\text{Stress Reduction}}{\text{Emotional Regulation}}$$

As Adin integrated mindfulness into his routine, he found that he could approach his activism with renewed vigor and clarity.

Additionally, Adin learned the importance of setting boundaries. He started to allocate specific times for activism and personal time, creating a schedule that honored both his commitments and his need for rest. This approach not only improved his mental health but also enhanced his effectiveness as an activist. By modeling healthy boundaries, Adin became an advocate for self-care within the LGBTQ community, encouraging others to prioritize their well-being alongside their activism.

Conclusion

The journey of balancing activism and self-care is fraught with challenges, as illustrated by Adin Xeris' experiences. Through the lens of compassion fatigue and burnout, we can better understand the emotional toll that activism can take. However, by adopting self-care strategies such as mindfulness and setting boundaries, activists like Adin can sustain their passion for justice while also nurturing their own health. In doing so, they not only empower themselves but also inspire others to recognize the importance of self-care in the ongoing fight for equality.

References:

+ Figley, C. R. (1995). *Compassion Fatigue: Coping with Secondary Traumatic Stress Disorder in Those Who Treat the Traumatized.*

+ Maslach, C., & Leiter, M. P. (2016). *Burnout: A Guide to Identifying Burnout and Pathways to Recovery.*

+ Goyal, M., Singh, S., Sibinga, E. M. S., & Shapiro, M. (2014). Meditation Programs for Psychological Stress and Well-Being: A Systematic Review and Meta-Analysis. *JAMA Internal Medicine*, 174(3), 357–368.

Battling anxiety and depression

Adin Xeris, like many activists, found that the weight of the world often pressed down on his shoulders. The struggle for LGBTQ rights was not just a fight for legal recognition but also an emotional battleground that could lead to anxiety and depression. In this section, we will explore the psychological toll of activism, the theories surrounding mental health, and Adin's personal journey through these turbulent waters.

The Psychological Toll of Activism

Activism can be a double-edged sword. On one hand, it offers purpose, community, and a sense of belonging; on the other, it can lead to burnout, anxiety, and depression. According to the *Stress-Buffering Model* (Cohen et al., 1997), social support can mitigate the effects of stress. However, when the fight for rights becomes overwhelming, even the most supportive communities can fall short.

Adin often felt the pressure of being a public figure in the LGBTQ movement. This pressure can lead to what is known as *Imposter Syndrome*, where individuals doubt their accomplishments and fear being exposed as a "fraud" (Clance & Imes, 1978). Adin questioned whether he was truly deserving of the accolades and recognition he received.

The Cycle of Anxiety and Depression

The cycle of anxiety and depression can be particularly vicious for activists. According to the *Cognitive Behavioral Theory* (Beck, 1976), negative thought patterns can lead to emotional distress. For Adin, the constant barrage of negative media coverage and opposition from conservative groups often triggered feelings of inadequacy.

$$\text{Anxiety} \rightarrow \text{Negative Thoughts} \rightarrow \text{Depression} \rightarrow \text{Increased Anxiety} \qquad (35)$$

This cycle made it difficult for him to focus on the positive changes he was advocating for. He often found himself trapped in a loop of despair, questioning the effectiveness of his efforts and whether the fight was worth the toll it took on his mental health.

Strategies for Coping

Recognizing the signs of anxiety and depression was the first step for Adin. He sought professional help, which is crucial for anyone battling mental health issues. The *World Health Organization* (WHO) emphasizes the importance of mental health care, stating that it is essential for overall well-being.

Adin also turned to mindfulness and meditation practices. Research has shown that mindfulness can significantly reduce symptoms of anxiety and depression (Kabat-Zinn, 1990). By focusing on the present moment and acknowledging his feelings without judgment, Adin began to find relief from the overwhelming pressures of activism.

$$\text{Mindfulness} \rightarrow \text{Increased Awareness} \rightarrow \text{Reduced Anxiety} \qquad (36)$$

In addition, Adin found solace in creative expression. Art, music, and writing became outlets for his emotions, allowing him to process his experiences in a healthy way. Engaging with the community through these creative avenues not only provided a therapeutic release but also connected him with others who shared similar struggles.

Building a Support Network

One of the most significant factors in Adin's journey was the importance of building a support network. Research shows that social connections can greatly enhance mental health (Berkman & Glass, 2000). Adin surrounded himself with friends, family, and fellow activists who understood the unique challenges faced by LGBTQ individuals.

He organized support groups within the LGBTQ community, creating safe spaces for individuals to share their experiences and feelings. These gatherings provided a platform for collective healing and empowerment, reinforcing the idea that no one is alone in their struggles.

Conclusion

Adin Xeris's battle with anxiety and depression highlights the importance of mental health awareness in activism. While the fight for LGBTQ rights is essential, it is equally important to prioritize self-care and seek help when needed. By embracing mindfulness, fostering supportive relationships, and expressing himself creatively, Adin was able to navigate the emotional challenges of activism. His journey serves as a reminder that even the most passionate advocates must care for their mental well-being to sustain their fight for equality.

In the end, Adin learned that vulnerability is not a weakness but a source of strength. Acknowledging his struggles allowed him to connect more deeply with others, fostering a sense of solidarity that would fuel his activism for years to come.

Seeking professional help for mental health

In the tumultuous journey of activism, mental health often takes a backseat, overshadowed by the pressing demands of the cause. For Adin Xeris, navigating the complexities of public advocacy while managing personal emotional turmoil became an increasingly daunting task. It is essential to recognize that seeking professional help is not a sign of weakness but a courageous step towards self-preservation and resilience.

Understanding the Need for Professional Help

The stigma surrounding mental health issues can be particularly pronounced in activist communities, where the pressure to appear strong and unyielding can lead individuals to neglect their own well-being. Adin, like many activists, grappled with feelings of anxiety and depression, exacerbated by the constant scrutiny and backlash faced from conservative factions in Tarvel.

Research indicates that activists are at a higher risk for mental health challenges due to the emotional toll of their work. According to a study by [?], individuals involved in social movements often experience heightened levels of stress, burnout, and compassion fatigue. These factors can lead to a cycle of mental health decline if left unaddressed.

Barriers to Seeking Help

Despite the pressing need for mental health support, several barriers can prevent activists like Adin from accessing professional help. These barriers include:

- **Stigma:** Fear of judgment from peers can deter individuals from seeking therapy.

- **Accessibility:** Limited access to mental health services, particularly in conservative areas like Tarvel, can make it challenging for activists to find appropriate care.

- **Financial Constraints:** The cost of therapy can be prohibitive, especially for those who may not have stable income due to their activist work.

Adin's initial reluctance to seek help stemmed from these barriers. He often thought, "How can I fight for others when I can't even handle my own issues?" This internal conflict is common among activists, who may prioritize their advocacy over their mental health.

The Turning Point: Embracing Therapy

Adin's journey towards seeking professional help began with a pivotal moment during a particularly challenging week of protests. After receiving a barrage of hateful messages online, Adin found himself spiraling into a deep state of anxiety. It was then that a close friend encouraged him to consider therapy, emphasizing that even the strongest warriors need support.

[?] highlights the importance of social support in mental health recovery, suggesting that having a trusted confidant can significantly impact an individual's willingness to seek help. With encouragement from his friend, Adin took the brave step to schedule his first therapy session.

In therapy, Adin discovered a safe space to unpack his feelings of inadequacy, fear, and exhaustion. His therapist introduced him to cognitive-behavioral techniques, which helped him reframe negative thoughts and develop coping strategies. For instance, they worked on the equation of stress management:

$$\text{Stress} = \text{Demands} - \text{Resources} \tag{37}$$

In this equation, the demands of activism often outweighed the resources available, leading to increased stress levels. Through therapy, Adin learned to identify and build his resources, such as self-care practices and community support, to mitigate the demands he faced.

The Benefits of Seeking Help

As Adin continued therapy, he noticed significant improvements in his mental health. He became more resilient, better equipped to handle the pressures of activism. The therapeutic process provided him with tools to manage anxiety and foster a healthier relationship with his work.

The benefits of seeking professional help are manifold:

+ **Improved Coping Mechanisms:** Therapy equips individuals with practical strategies to deal with stress and anxiety.

+ **Enhanced Self-Awareness:** Through therapy, Adin gained insights into his triggers and emotional responses, allowing him to navigate challenging situations more effectively.

+ **Increased Empathy:** By addressing his own mental health, Adin became more empathetic towards others in the community facing similar struggles.

Adin's advocacy work flourished as he embraced his mental health journey. He began to openly share his experiences with therapy, aiming to destigmatize mental health discussions within the LGBTQ community. This openness encouraged others to seek help, fostering a culture of support and understanding.

Conclusion: The Ongoing Journey

Adin Xeris's story illustrates the importance of seeking professional help for mental health, particularly within the demanding realm of activism. By prioritizing his mental well-being, Adin not only enhanced his capacity to fight for LGBTQ rights but also inspired countless others to do the same.

In a world that often demands relentless resilience, it is crucial to remember that seeking help is a vital act of self-care. As Adin learned, the journey towards mental health is ongoing, and it is one that every activist can embark upon, leading to a more sustainable and impactful fight for equality.

Inspiring others to prioritize mental well-being

In the midst of the fervent battles for LGBTQ rights, Adin Xeris recognized that activism extended beyond the streets and legislative halls; it also resided deeply within the psyche of individuals. Mental well-being, often overshadowed by the immediate demands of social justice, became a cornerstone of Adin's advocacy. This section delves into how Adin inspired others to prioritize mental health, drawing on relevant theories, challenges, and impactful examples.

Understanding Mental Health in Activism

The intersection of mental health and activism is crucial, as activists often face unique stressors including societal backlash, personal identity struggles, and the weight of representing marginalized communities. According to the *Ecological Model of Health*, individuals exist within multiple layers of influence, from personal to societal. This model emphasizes that mental well-being is not solely an individual concern but is affected by broader social contexts.

$$M = f(P, E) \tag{38}$$

where M is mental well-being, P represents personal factors (such as resilience and coping strategies), and E encapsulates environmental influences (including community support and societal attitudes).

Adin's approach to mental health advocacy was multifaceted, focusing on both personal resilience and community support systems.

The Problems Faced

Adin encountered several challenges in promoting mental well-being among LGBTQ activists. Stigma surrounding mental health issues often deterred individuals from seeking help. Many felt that acknowledging mental struggles would undermine their credibility as activists. Furthermore, the pervasive culture of "hustle" within activist circles often glorified burnout, leading to a cycle of neglecting self-care.

$$B = \frac{E}{R} \tag{39}$$

Here, B denotes burnout, E represents effort exerted in activism, and R signifies personal resources. As activists pushed themselves harder without adequate support, burnout rates soared, impacting mental health and activism efficacy.

Adin's Initiatives

To counteract these issues, Adin launched several initiatives aimed at fostering mental well-being among activists:

+ **Workshops and Support Groups:** Adin organized workshops focused on mental health literacy, where participants learned about the importance of self-care, resilience, and coping mechanisms. Support groups were established to create safe spaces for sharing experiences and feelings.

+ **Mental Health Days:** Recognizing the toll of continuous activism, Adin advocated for designated mental health days within activist organizations. These days encouraged individuals to step back, recharge, and focus on their well-being without guilt.

+ **Collaboration with Mental Health Professionals:** Adin partnered with mental health professionals to provide resources and counseling to activists. This collaboration aimed to bridge the gap between activism and mental health support.

Real-Life Examples

One poignant example of Adin's impact came during the planning of the first LGBTQ Awareness March in Tarvel. As excitement built, so did anxiety among organizers. Adin introduced a "mental health check-in" at every planning meeting. This practice not only normalized discussions about mental health but also fostered a supportive environment where individuals felt safe expressing their struggles.

Another notable instance was during a national conference where Adin spoke candidly about their own mental health challenges. By sharing their story of battling anxiety and depression, Adin dismantled the stigma surrounding mental health in the activist community. Attendees reported feeling empowered to seek help and prioritize their mental well-being, inspired by Adin's vulnerability and authenticity.

Theoretical Frameworks Supporting Mental Well-being

Adin's advocacy was also rooted in various psychological theories that emphasize the importance of mental health in overall well-being. The *Positive Psychology* movement, championed by figures like Martin Seligman, posits that focusing on strengths and fostering positive emotions can enhance resilience and coping skills. Adin incorporated these principles into their workshops, encouraging activists to celebrate small victories and cultivate gratitude.

Furthermore, the *Social Identity Theory* highlights how individuals derive a sense of self from their group memberships. Adin emphasized the importance of community support in bolstering mental health, encouraging activists to lean on their chosen families for emotional sustenance.

Conclusion

Adin Xeris's commitment to inspiring others to prioritize mental well-being became a pivotal aspect of their legacy. By intertwining mental health advocacy with LGBTQ activism, Adin illuminated the path for future activists to navigate the complexities of their identities while maintaining their mental health. Their work not only transformed the activist landscape in Tarvel but also set a precedent for recognizing mental well-being as an integral component of social justice movements.

As the fight for LGBTQ rights continues, the lessons learned from Adin's advocacy serve as a reminder that self-care is not a luxury but a necessity. In the words of Adin, "You can't pour from an empty cup; fill yourself first, and then you can fill the world."

Family and Acceptance

Reconciling with Conservative Family Members

Reconciling with conservative family members can be one of the most challenging aspects of an LGBTQ activist's journey, particularly for someone like Adin Xeris, who grew up in a conservative environment in Tarvel. This section explores the complexities of familial relationships, the theory behind acceptance and reconciliation, and real-life examples that illustrate the struggles and triumphs faced by individuals in similar situations.

Theoretical Framework

The process of reconciling with conservative family members often involves navigating through various psychological theories, including the *Stages of Change Model* (Prochaska & DiClemente, 1983). This model outlines five stages: precontemplation, contemplation, preparation, action, and maintenance. Understanding these stages can provide insight into how both the activist and their family members can evolve in their understanding and acceptance of LGBTQ identities.

$$\text{Stages of Change: } S = \{P, C, Pr, A, M\} \tag{40}$$

where S represents the stages, P is precontemplation, C is contemplation, Pr is preparation, A is action, and M is maintenance.

The Problems Faced

1.   **Cultural and Religious Beliefs**: Many conservative families hold deep-rooted beliefs that may conflict with LGBTQ identities. These beliefs often stem from cultural, religious, or societal norms that view homosexuality as a taboo. For instance, Adin's family may have grown up in a community where traditional gender roles and heterosexual relationships were the norm, leading to initial resistance when confronted with his identity.

   2. **Fear of Change**: Family members may fear that accepting an LGBTQ identity means they must reevaluate their own beliefs and values. This fear can manifest as denial, anger, or withdrawal, making reconciliation difficult. Adin's experience of coming out might have been met with shock, leading to a temporary rift as family members grappled with their emotions.

3. **Miscommunication**: A lack of understanding about LGBTQ issues can lead to miscommunication. Family members may rely on stereotypes or misinformation, which can create barriers to meaningful dialogue. Adin's attempts to explain his identity may have been met with skepticism or misunderstanding, further complicating the reconciliation process.

Strategies for Reconciliation

1. **Open Dialogue**: Establishing open lines of communication is crucial. Adin could initiate conversations with his family, expressing his feelings and experiences in a way that invites empathy. For example, sharing personal stories about discrimination or the importance of love and acceptance can humanize the LGBTQ experience for conservative family members.

2. **Education**: Providing resources and information about LGBTQ issues can help demystify misconceptions. Adin might recommend books, documentaries, or articles that present LGBTQ narratives in a relatable manner. This educational approach can facilitate understanding and reduce fear.

3. **Patience and Persistence**: Reconciliation is often a gradual process. Adin would need to exercise patience as his family navigates their feelings. Celebrating small victories, such as a family member expressing curiosity or willingness to learn, can motivate continued efforts toward acceptance.

4. **Finding Common Ground**: Identifying shared values can help bridge the gap between differing perspectives. Adin might emphasize universal themes such as love, family, and acceptance, framing his identity as an extension of these values rather than a deviation from them.

Real-Life Examples

Many LGBTQ activists have faced similar challenges with their conservative families. For instance, the story of *David*, a gay man from a conservative background, illustrates the potential for reconciliation. After coming out, David's parents struggled to accept his identity, often resorting to silence during family gatherings. However, through persistent dialogue and sharing his experiences, David gradually shifted their perspective. Over time, his parents began to attend LGBTQ events and even joined local advocacy efforts, demonstrating that change is possible with patience and understanding.

Another example is *Maria*, a transgender activist, who faced rejection from her family upon coming out. Initially, her parents refused to acknowledge her identity. However, after Maria organized a family meeting where she shared her journey and the struggles faced by transgender individuals, her parents began to understand the importance of acceptance. They eventually became advocates for LGBTQ rights within their community, showcasing the transformative power of education and dialogue.

Conclusion

Reconciling with conservative family members is a complex and often painful journey for LGBTQ activists like Adin Xeris. By employing strategies such as open dialogue, education, patience, and finding common ground, activists can foster understanding and acceptance within their families. While the path to reconciliation may be fraught with challenges, the stories of individuals who have successfully navigated this terrain serve as powerful reminders that love and acceptance can ultimately prevail.

$$\text{Reconciliation Success} = f(\text{Dialogue, Education, Patience, Common Ground})$$
$$(41)$$

where f represents the function of reconciliation success based on the aforementioned factors.

The supportive LGBTQ community as a chosen family

In the journey of self-discovery and acceptance, many individuals within the LGBTQ community find themselves seeking solace and support outside their biological families. This phenomenon is often referred to as "chosen family," a concept that encapsulates the deep bonds formed among individuals who share similar experiences, struggles, and identities. For Adin Xeris, the supportive LGBTQ community became not just a refuge, but a vital source of strength and empowerment.

The theory of chosen family is rooted in the understanding that familial bonds are not solely defined by blood relations. According to [?], the concept of chosen family allows individuals to create supportive networks that fulfill emotional and psychological needs often unmet by traditional family structures. This is particularly relevant for LGBTQ individuals who may face rejection or lack of understanding from their biological families due to their sexual orientation or gender identity.

The Importance of Chosen Family

Adin's experience illustrates the profound impact that a chosen family can have on one's mental health and overall well-being. In Tarvel, where conservative values often dominated social interactions, finding acceptance was a challenging endeavor. However, through local LGBTQ gatherings, Adin encountered others who shared similar stories of struggle and triumph. These interactions led to the formation of deep friendships that transcended mere acquaintance; they became a lifeline.

The support offered by chosen families can manifest in various ways, including emotional support, financial assistance, and a sense of belonging. For instance, during moments of crisis, such as when Adin faced backlash from conservative groups, his chosen family rallied around him, providing not only moral support but also practical help in organizing events and campaigns. This solidarity is crucial in fostering resilience among LGBTQ individuals, as illustrated by the work of [?], who discusses the role of social support in mitigating the effects of stigma and discrimination.

Challenges and Resilience

However, the journey to finding a chosen family is not without its challenges. Many LGBTQ individuals experience initial feelings of isolation and loneliness, particularly in environments that are not affirming. The fear of rejection can prevent individuals from seeking out community connections. Adin himself faced these hurdles, battling the internalized stigma that often accompanies growing up in a conservative town like Tarvel.

Moreover, the dynamics within chosen families can be complex. Conflicts may arise due to differing opinions, backgrounds, or experiences. Yet, these conflicts can also lead to growth and understanding, as members learn to navigate their differences in a supportive environment. Adin's advocacy for open communication and acceptance within his chosen family not only strengthened their bonds but also fostered a culture of inclusivity that extended beyond their immediate circle.

Examples of Chosen Family in Action

Adin's activism was greatly influenced by the support he received from his chosen family. One notable example was during the organization of the first LGBTQ Awareness March in Tarvel. Adin's chosen family played a pivotal role in mobilizing the community, ensuring that the event was not only well-attended but also a safe space for expression. They provided logistical support, helped with fundraising, and most importantly, brought a sense of joy and celebration to what could have been a daunting task.

This event exemplified the power of chosen family as a source of strength and resilience. The march not only raised awareness but also solidified the bonds among participants, many of whom had never felt a sense of belonging before. The laughter, camaraderie, and shared purpose created an atmosphere that resonated deeply with all involved.

Conclusion

In conclusion, the supportive LGBTQ community serves as a chosen family for many individuals, providing essential emotional and social support. For Adin Xeris, this community was instrumental in his journey toward self-acceptance and activism. By fostering connections based on shared experiences and mutual understanding, chosen families play a critical role in the lives of LGBTQ individuals, enabling them to thrive in the face of adversity. As the fight for equality continues, the importance of these chosen families cannot be overstated; they represent not only resilience but also the profound human need for connection and acceptance.

Honoring LGBTQ elders and empowering youth

In the vibrant tapestry of the LGBTQ community, the threads of history are woven by the voices of both our elders and our youth. Honoring LGBTQ elders is not just a matter of respect; it is a vital component of our identity and activism. These individuals have fought battles that many of us today can scarcely imagine, paving the way for the rights and freedoms we enjoy. Their stories, struggles, and triumphs form the foundation upon which the current generation stands.

The Importance of Elders in the LGBTQ Community

Elders in the LGBTQ community serve as living libraries of experience and wisdom. They are the bearers of stories that encapsulate the evolution of our rights, culture, and community. According to the theory of intergenerational solidarity, the exchange of knowledge and support between generations strengthens community bonds and enhances resilience [?]. This solidarity is crucial, especially in times of crisis, where the lessons learned from past struggles can inform current strategies for advocacy.

For instance, the Stonewall Riots of 1969 marked a significant turning point in the fight for LGBTQ rights. Elders who lived through this era often recount the raw emotions, the sense of urgency, and the community spirit that fueled the movement. Their narratives remind younger activists of the sacrifices made and the importance of perseverance. By honoring these stories, we not only preserve our history but also inspire the next generation to continue the fight for equality.

Empowering Youth: A Two-Way Street

Empowering youth in the LGBTQ community involves equipping them with the tools, resources, and confidence to become effective advocates for their rights. However, this empowerment is a two-way street; it also requires engaging with and learning from our elders. As the famous activist Marsha P. Johnson once said, "No pride for some of us without liberation for all of us." This sentiment underscores the necessity of collaboration between generations.

Youth empowerment can take various forms, including mentorship programs, workshops, and community organizing. For example, programs that pair young activists with seasoned advocates can facilitate the transfer of knowledge and skills. This mentorship not only helps youth navigate the complexities of activism but also fosters a sense of belonging and community.

Moreover, the concept of "youth-led movements" has gained traction in recent years, emphasizing the importance of young voices in shaping the future of LGBTQ advocacy. Organizations like the *Youth Pride Alliance* have demonstrated the effectiveness of youth-led initiatives, providing platforms for young LGBTQ individuals to express their concerns and advocate for change.

Challenges Faced by LGBTQ Youth and Elders

Despite the progress made, both LGBTQ youth and elders face unique challenges that can hinder their empowerment. LGBTQ youth often encounter issues such as bullying, discrimination, and mental health struggles. According to the *Trevor Project*, LGBTQ youth are more than twice as likely to experience bullying compared to their heterosexual peers [?]. These challenges can lead to feelings of isolation and despair, making it imperative for the community to provide robust support systems.

On the other hand, LGBTQ elders frequently grapple with issues of invisibility and marginalization. As they age, many find themselves disconnected from the younger generation, leading to a loss of their voices in the ongoing dialogue about LGBTQ rights. This disconnection can be exacerbated by societal ageism, which often overlooks the contributions of older individuals in favor of youth-centric narratives.

Bridging the Generational Gap

To bridge the generational gap, it is essential to create spaces where both elders and youth can come together to share experiences, learn from one another, and collaborate on activism. Community centers, pride events, and intergenerational workshops can serve as platforms for these exchanges.

For example, the *Generations Project* is an initiative that brings together LGBTQ elders and youth to engage in storytelling and advocacy. Participants share their experiences, discuss the evolution of LGBTQ rights, and brainstorm strategies for future activism. Such initiatives not only honor the contributions of elders but also empower youth by instilling a sense of purpose and connection to their community's history.

Conclusion

In conclusion, honoring LGBTQ elders and empowering youth is a fundamental aspect of building a resilient and inclusive community. By recognizing the invaluable contributions of our elders and actively engaging with our youth, we can create a powerful intergenerational alliance that strengthens our collective voice. As we continue to fight for equality, let us remember that our history is not just a series of events; it is a living narrative that connects us all. By working together, we can ensure that the legacy of our elders inspires the next generation to carry the torch of activism forward.

Adin's Legacy

Adin's Legacy

Adin's Legacy

Adin Xeris stands as a beacon of hope and resilience in the fight for LGBTQ rights, embodying the struggles and triumphs of countless individuals who have fought for equality. This chapter delves into the profound impact of Adin's activism, exploring the ways in which he catalyzed change in public perception, influenced legislation, and inspired future generations.

Section 1: The Impact of Adin's Activism

Adin's activism can be understood through various theoretical frameworks that examine social movements and their effects on societal norms. One such theory is the **Framing Theory**, which posits that the way issues are presented can significantly influence public perception and mobilization. Adin effectively framed LGBTQ rights as a matter of human dignity and civil rights, thus garnering broader support across diverse communities.

$$\text{Public Support} \propto \text{Visibility} \times \text{Framing} \tag{42}$$

This equation suggests that public support for LGBTQ rights is directly proportional to the visibility of the issues and the effectiveness of the framing employed by activists. Adin's strategic use of media, personal storytelling, and public demonstrations brought LGBTQ issues into the mainstream, challenging stereotypes and misconceptions.

Subsection 1: Changing Public Perception on LGBTQ Rights

Before Adin's emergence as a public figure, LGBTQ issues were often marginalized or misrepresented in mainstream discourse. Through his tireless efforts, Adin played a pivotal role in reshaping narratives surrounding LGBTQ identities. For instance, his participation in the first LGBTQ Awareness March in Tarvel drew significant media attention, showcasing the vibrant diversity of the community. The event not only attracted local supporters but also garnered national coverage, shifting the narrative from one of shame to one of pride.

$$\text{Media Attention} = f(\text{Event Size, Public Sentiment}) \tag{43}$$

Here, f represents a function that captures how media attention is influenced by the size of the event and prevailing public sentiment. Adin's ability to mobilize a large crowd demonstrated the strength of community solidarity, which in turn positively influenced public sentiment toward LGBTQ issues.

Subsection 2: Influencing National Legislation for Equality

Adin's activism transcended local boundaries, impacting national legislation aimed at securing LGBTQ rights. His lobbying efforts were instrumental in the passage of anti-discrimination laws and the challenge against Tarvel's marriage equality ban. By collaborating with established advocacy groups, Adin was able to leverage their resources and networks, amplifying his voice in the corridors of power.

$$\text{Legislative Change} = \text{Advocacy Efforts} + \text{Public Support} \tag{44}$$

This equation illustrates that legislative change is a product of organized advocacy efforts combined with public support. Adin's ability to rally support from the community was crucial in creating a conducive environment for legislative change, demonstrating that grassroots activism can lead to significant policy shifts.

Subsection 3: Inspiring Future Generations of Activists

One of the most enduring aspects of Adin's legacy is his ability to inspire future generations of activists. His story serves as a powerful reminder that change is possible, even in the face of adversity. Adin frequently mentored young activists, sharing his experiences and strategies for effective advocacy. This mentorship not only empowered individuals but also fostered a sense of community and continuity within the movement.

$$\text{Inspiration} = \text{Mentorship} \times \text{Visibility of Role Models} \qquad (45)$$

In this context, inspiration is amplified by the presence of mentors and visible role models like Adin. His commitment to uplifting others ensured that the fight for equality would continue long after his time, creating a legacy of activism that transcended generations.

Subsection 4: Adin's Journey from Pariah to Icon

Adin's transformation from a closeted individual in a conservative town to a celebrated activist is a testament to the power of resilience and authenticity. Initially viewed as a pariah, Adin faced significant backlash from conservative groups. However, through his unwavering commitment to his cause, he gradually shifted perceptions, ultimately becoming an icon of the LGBTQ movement.

$$\text{Icon Status} = \text{Public Acceptance} + \text{Cultural Impact} \qquad (46)$$

This equation suggests that an individual's status as an icon is dependent on both public acceptance and their cultural impact. Adin's ability to connect with diverse audiences through humor, vulnerability, and relatability contributed to his rise as a cultural icon, solidifying his place in LGBTQ history.

Conclusion

Adin Xeris's legacy is a multifaceted tapestry woven from the threads of activism, resilience, and inspiration. His impact on public perception, legislative change, and the empowerment of future generations underscores the importance of visibility and advocacy in the ongoing struggle for LGBTQ rights. As society continues to evolve, Adin's story serves as a guiding light, reminding us that the fight for equality is far from over and that each of us has a role to play in this critical journey.

In reflecting on Adin's legacy, it is essential to recognize that the journey toward equality requires continuous effort and commitment. As we honor his contributions, we must also strive to carry forward the torch of activism, ensuring that the ideals for which Adin fought remain alive and vibrant in our communities.

The Impact of Adin's Activism

Changing public perception on LGBTQ rights

The journey towards changing public perception on LGBTQ rights has been a complex interplay of social dynamics, cultural shifts, and relentless activism. In Tarvel, where conservative values often reigned supreme, the transformation of societal attitudes towards LGBTQ individuals was not just a goal; it was a necessity for the survival and flourishing of a marginalized community.

Theoretical Framework

To understand this shift, we can draw on social change theories, particularly the Social Movement Theory. This theory posits that social movements arise in response to perceived injustices, aiming to create change through collective action. The LGBTQ movement in Tarvel exemplified this, as activists like Adin Xeris rallied individuals to challenge the status quo.

The process of changing public perception can be modeled using the **Diffusion of Innovations** theory proposed by Rogers (1962). This theory outlines how new ideas and practices spread within a society, emphasizing the roles of innovators, early adopters, early majority, late majority, and laggards. In Tarvel, the innovators were the brave individuals who came out publicly, while the early adopters included allies who began to advocate for LGBTQ rights.

$$P(t) = \frac{N}{1 + \left(\frac{N - P_0}{P_0}\right) e^{-kt}} \tag{47}$$

Where:

+ $P(t)$ = the number of individuals adopting the innovation at time t,

+ N = the maximum number of potential adopters,

+ P_0 = the initial number of adopters,

+ k = the rate of adoption.

This equation illustrates how as time progresses, the number of individuals accepting LGBTQ rights increases, reflecting a shift in public perception.

Challenges Faced

Despite the theoretical frameworks that explain social change, the path to altering public perception was fraught with challenges. In Tarvel, conservative backlash was a significant obstacle. Many individuals held deep-seated beliefs rooted in traditional values, often fueled by misinformation and stereotypes about LGBTQ individuals.

For instance, when Adin organized the first LGBTQ Awareness March in Tarvel, it was met with fierce opposition from conservative groups. Protesters wielded signs with slogans like "Protect Our Children" and "Family Values Matter," which served to instill fear and perpetuate harmful narratives about LGBTQ individuals. This backlash highlighted the need for strategic communication and education to counteract misinformation.

Strategies for Change

To combat these challenges, Adin and fellow activists employed various strategies aimed at reshaping public perception.

- + **Storytelling:** Personal narratives played a crucial role in humanizing LGBTQ issues. Adin shared his journey of self-discovery and the struggles he faced in a conservative environment. By putting a face to the movement, he was able to foster empathy and understanding among those who might have previously held prejudiced views.

- + **Visibility:** Increasing the visibility of LGBTQ individuals in public spaces was another effective tactic. Adin encouraged local LGBTQ members to share their stories through community events, art, and social media. This visibility challenged stereotypes and demonstrated that LGBTQ individuals were not "other," but integral members of the Tarvel community.

- + **Education Campaigns:** Adin spearheaded educational initiatives aimed at dispelling myths about LGBTQ individuals. Workshops in schools, community centers, and local churches provided a platform for dialogue and learning. These efforts were crucial in shifting perceptions among the youth and conservative adults alike.

Impact of Media and Pop Culture

The role of media and pop culture cannot be overlooked in this narrative. As LGBTQ representation in film, television, and literature increased, so too did public awareness and acceptance. Shows like *Will & Grace* and *Pose* not only entertained but also educated audiences about LGBTQ lives, challenges, and triumphs.

In Tarvel, local media began to cover LGBTQ events more positively, showcasing the human stories behind the activism. This shift in coverage was pivotal in altering the narrative from one of fear and misunderstanding to one of celebration and acceptance.

Examples of Change

The culmination of these efforts was evident in several key moments. For instance, the successful organization of the first LGBTQ Awareness March in Tarvel drew a crowd of over a thousand supporters, including allies from various backgrounds. This event marked a significant turning point, demonstrating that public support for LGBTQ rights was growing.

Moreover, as Adin became a leading activist, he was invited to speak at national LGBTQ conferences, amplifying the voice of Tarvel's LGBTQ community. His speeches often highlighted the importance of grassroots activism and the need for solidarity across communities.

Conclusion

Changing public perception on LGBTQ rights in Tarvel was not an overnight success; it was a gradual process marked by resilience, creativity, and unwavering commitment to justice. Through the combined efforts of individuals like Adin Xeris and the broader LGBTQ community, Tarvel witnessed a transformation that not only advanced LGBTQ rights but also enriched the social fabric of the entire community.

As we reflect on this journey, it becomes clear that the fight for LGBTQ rights is ongoing. The lessons learned from Tarvel serve as a reminder that changing hearts and minds requires patience, empathy, and a collective effort to build a more inclusive society for all.

Influencing national legislation for equality

In the throes of a rapidly changing social landscape, Adin Xeris emerged as a formidable force in the fight for LGBTQ+ rights, particularly in influencing national legislation aimed at equality. His journey was not merely a personal endeavor; it was a collective movement that sought to dismantle systemic barriers and promote inclusivity across the nation. This section delves into the strategies employed by Adin and the LGBTQ+ community to effect change at the legislative level, the challenges they faced, and the tangible impacts of their efforts.

Theoretical Framework

To understand the significance of Adin's activism in influencing national legislation, we must consider the theoretical underpinnings of social movements. According to Charles Tilly's theory of contentious politics, social movements are crucial in shaping political outcomes by mobilizing resources, framing issues, and constructing collective identities. Adin's activism can be viewed through this lens, as he utilized various strategies to mobilize support and frame LGBTQ+ rights as a fundamental issue of human rights.

$$P = \frac{R + C + M}{S} \tag{48}$$

Where:

+ P = Political power achieved

+ R = Resources mobilized (financial, human, informational)

+ C = Collective identity and solidarity among the LGBTQ+ community

+ M = Media attention and public support

+ S = Structural barriers to change (e.g., conservative legislation, institutional resistance)

Adin's ability to influence national legislation can be seen as a function of these variables, where the mobilization of resources and the creation of a collective identity played pivotal roles in overcoming structural barriers.

Mobilizing Resources

One of the first steps Adin took in influencing national legislation was the mobilization of resources. This included not only financial support but also the recruitment of volunteers and activists. Adin organized fundraising events, such as the "Tarvel Pride Gala," which attracted local businesses and national sponsors. The funds raised were crucial for lobbying efforts and the establishment of a robust advocacy group.

$$F = \sum_{i=1}^{n} S_i \qquad (49)$$

Where:

+ F = Total funds raised

+ S_i = Contributions from individual sponsors or events

+ n = Number of fundraising events or sponsors

Through these efforts, Adin was able to gather significant financial resources that were instrumental in hiring lobbyists and legal experts who could navigate the complexities of the legislative process.

Framing the Issue

Adin understood the importance of framing LGBTQ+ rights as a matter of civil rights rather than a niche issue. By aligning the struggle for LGBTQ+ equality with broader themes of justice and human rights, he was able to attract a diverse coalition of supporters. This approach was evident in his speeches, where he often invoked historical civil rights movements, drawing parallels that resonated with a wider audience.

$$I = \frac{R_f}{R_t} \qquad (50)$$

Where:

+ I = Impact of the framing

+ R_f = Resources mobilized through effective framing

+ R_t = Total resources available for the cause

This framing not only garnered public sympathy but also pressured lawmakers to reconsider their stances on LGBTQ+ issues, recognizing that opposition could be seen as a violation of fundamental rights.

Legislative Advocacy and Lobbying

With resources in hand and a compelling narrative, Adin and his team embarked on a lobbying campaign aimed at influencing key legislators. They organized meetings with congressional representatives, providing them with data and personal stories that highlighted the necessity of anti-discrimination laws and marriage equality.

One pivotal moment came when Adin organized a delegation of LGBTQ+ individuals to meet with lawmakers in Washington, D.C. This grassroots effort demonstrated the real-life implications of legislative decisions, making the abstract concept of equality tangible. The emotional testimonies of individuals who faced discrimination were particularly impactful, leading to increased support among undecided lawmakers.

Challenges and Backlash

Despite their successes, Adin and the LGBTQ+ community faced significant challenges. Conservative groups mobilized in opposition, often resorting to fear-based tactics to sway public opinion against LGBTQ+ rights. This backlash manifested in attempts to introduce legislation that would undermine the progress made, such as "religious freedom" laws that allowed discrimination under the guise of religious beliefs.

Adin's response to this backlash was strategic. He emphasized the importance of unity within the LGBTQ+ community and allied groups, calling for a coordinated response to counteract misinformation. This included social media campaigns, public demonstrations, and collaborations with other marginalized communities to amplify their voices.

Tangible Impacts

The culmination of Adin's efforts and those of the LGBTQ+ community led to significant legislative victories. Notably, the passage of the Equality Act, which aimed to prohibit discrimination based on sexual orientation and gender identity in various sectors, was a landmark achievement. This legislation not only represented a victory for LGBTQ+ rights but also served as a template for other nations grappling with similar issues.

$$C = \frac{V_{after} - V_{before}}{V_{before}} \times 100 \tag{51}$$

Where:

- C = Change in public sentiment

- V_{after} = Public support after legislative changes

- V_{before} = Public support before legislative changes

Studies indicated a notable increase in public support for LGBTQ+ rights following the passage of the Equality Act, demonstrating the effectiveness of Adin's advocacy and the community's resilience.

Conclusion

Adin Xeris' influence on national legislation for LGBTQ+ equality exemplifies the power of grassroots activism in shaping political landscapes. Through strategic resource mobilization, effective framing, and persistent advocacy, he was able to challenge the status quo and drive significant change. The journey was fraught with challenges, but the resilience of Adin and the LGBTQ+ community paved the way for a more inclusive future. As we reflect on these efforts, it is essential to recognize that the fight for equality is ongoing, and the lessons learned from Adin's activism continue to inspire new generations of advocates.

Inspiring future generations of activists

In the wake of Adin Xeris' formidable journey as an LGBTQ activist, the question arises: how can one individual's legacy inspire future generations of activists? The answer lies in the multifaceted approach Adin took to activism, which can be distilled into several core principles that resonate with emerging leaders in social justice movements today.

1. The Power of Visibility

Adin's journey underscored the importance of visibility in activism. By bravely sharing his story, he not only brought attention to the struggles faced by LGBTQ individuals in Tarvel but also created a sense of belonging for those who felt marginalized. The theory of *social identity* posits that individuals derive a sense of self from their group memberships, which can be particularly powerful in movements seeking equality. Adin's visibility served as a beacon, encouraging others to embrace their identities and advocate for their rights.

$$\text{Visibility} = \text{Self-Acceptance} + \text{Community Engagement} \qquad (52)$$

This equation illustrates how visibility is a product of both personal acceptance and active participation in community efforts. Future activists can learn from Adin's example by recognizing that their stories have the potential to inspire others who may be struggling with their identities.

2. Mentorship and Empowerment

Another significant aspect of Adin's legacy was his commitment to mentorship. By actively engaging with younger activists, Adin fostered an environment where knowledge and experience could be shared. The *mentorship theory* suggests that mentorship not only benefits the mentee but also reinforces the mentor's own understanding and commitment to their cause.

Adin's mentorship initiatives included workshops, public speaking engagements, and informal gatherings where young activists could ask questions and share their experiences. This approach not only empowered the next generation but also created a supportive network that encouraged collaboration and innovation.

$$\text{Empowerment} = \text{Knowledge Transfer} + \text{Support Networks} \qquad (53)$$

This equation highlights the dual components of empowerment in activism: the sharing of knowledge and the establishment of supportive relationships. Adin's legacy serves as a reminder that fostering the growth of future leaders is essential for the sustainability of any movement.

3. Intersectionality in Activism

Adin's activism was grounded in the principle of intersectionality, recognizing that the struggles faced by LGBTQ individuals are often compounded by other social identities, such as race, class, and gender. This understanding is crucial for inspiring future activists to adopt a holistic approach to advocacy.

Kimberlé Crenshaw, who coined the term *intersectionality*, emphasizes that social justice movements must address the interconnected nature of social categorizations. Adin's ability to articulate the need for inclusivity within the LGBTQ movement serves as a powerful model for future leaders.

$$\text{Advocacy} = \text{Inclusion} \times \text{Intersectionality} \qquad (54)$$

This equation encapsulates the idea that effective advocacy is amplified when it incorporates diverse perspectives and experiences. Adin's legacy encourages future activists to consider the broader social context in which they operate, ensuring that their efforts are inclusive and equitable.

4. Creative Expression as a Tool for Change

Adin also recognized the power of creative expression in activism. Through art, music, and storytelling, he was able to communicate complex issues in an accessible manner. The *cultural theory of social movements* posits that cultural expressions can mobilize communities and inspire action.

Adin's engagement with local artists and creators fostered a vibrant culture of activism in Tarvel, where creative projects became platforms for dialogue and awareness. By encouraging future activists to harness their creativity, Adin demonstrated that art can be a potent catalyst for social change.

$$\text{Cultural Mobilization} = \text{Artistic Expression} + \text{Community Engagement} \quad (55)$$

This equation emphasizes that cultural mobilization thrives when artistic expression is coupled with active community involvement. Adin's legacy inspires future activists to explore innovative methods of communication that resonate with diverse audiences.

5. Resilience and Adaptability

Finally, Adin's journey exemplified the importance of resilience and adaptability in activism. The challenges he faced—from opposition to personal struggles—required a steadfast commitment to his cause. The *resilience theory* posits that the ability to bounce back from adversity is crucial for long-term success in any endeavor.

Future activists can draw inspiration from Adin's ability to navigate setbacks while maintaining a clear vision for change. His story serves as a reminder that resilience is not just about enduring hardship, but also about adapting strategies to meet evolving challenges.

$$\text{Resilience} = \text{Adaptability} + \text{Commitment} \quad (56)$$

This equation illustrates that resilience in activism is a combination of being adaptable to changing circumstances and maintaining a strong commitment to one's goals. Adin's legacy encourages future leaders to embrace challenges as opportunities for growth and innovation.

Conclusion

In summary, Adin Xeris' legacy as an LGBTQ activist provides a rich framework for inspiring future generations. By emphasizing visibility, mentorship, intersectionality, creative expression, and resilience, Adin's journey serves as a powerful model for emerging activists. As they continue to battle for equality and justice, the principles embodied in Adin's activism will undoubtedly guide and empower them in their own pursuits. The future of activism is bright, fueled by the enduring spirit of those who came before and the promise of those yet to come.

Adin's journey from pariah to icon

Adin Xeris's transformation from a pariah to an icon is a tale that resonates deeply within the LGBTQ+ community and beyond. It is a journey marked by resilience, courage, and an unwavering commitment to equality. At the outset, Adin was viewed as an outcast in the conservative town of Tarvel, where traditional values dominated the cultural landscape. This section explores the complexities of Adin's evolution and the socio-political dynamics that facilitated this remarkable transformation.

The Initial Struggles

In the early days of his activism, Adin faced significant backlash from his community. The conservative values prevalent in Tarvel fostered an environment where being different was met with hostility. Adin's initial forays into LGBTQ advocacy were met with scorn, ridicule, and even threats. This societal rejection is a common theme in the lives of many activists, where the courage to stand up for one's identity often leads to isolation.

$$\text{Social Rejection} = f(\text{Identity} + \text{Activism}) \qquad (57)$$

In this equation, social rejection is a function of one's identity and the act of activism. As Adin began to embrace his identity and advocate for LGBTQ rights, he experienced the full force of societal rejection, which further fueled his determination to change the narrative.

Finding Strength in Community

However, it was through the very act of fighting back that Adin found his community. The LGBTQ+ individuals he connected with became his support system, transforming his loneliness into solidarity. This phenomenon is often described in social movement theory as the "collective identity," where individuals unite under a shared experience of marginalization.

Adin's underground gatherings became a sanctuary for those who felt similarly ostracized. These meetings were not just about sharing struggles; they were a celebration of identity. Adin's charisma and passion began to draw attention, turning him from a mere participant into a leader.

The Turning Point

The turning point in Adin's journey came during the first LGBTQ Awareness March in Tarvel. What started as a small gathering quickly escalated into a significant event that caught the eye of local media. The march was both a statement and a spectacle, showcasing the vibrant spirit of the LGBTQ community in a town that had long suppressed it.

$$\text{Visibility} = \text{Media Attention} \times \text{Public Engagement} \tag{58}$$

This equation illustrates that increased visibility is a product of media attention and public engagement. As Adin led the march, he became the face of a movement that was previously invisible in Tarvel. The media coverage not only amplified his message but also began to shift public perception.

From Controversy to Recognition

As Adin gained recognition, he also faced controversies that challenged his newfound status. Criticism from conservative groups intensified, painting him as a radical. However, Adin's ability to navigate these challenges showcased his resilience. He adeptly used the controversies to further his cause, turning negative narratives into opportunities for dialogue.

$$\text{Activist Reputation} = \text{Public Perception} + \text{Controversy Management} \tag{59}$$

Adin's reputation as an activist grew as he learned to manage controversies effectively. This skill became instrumental in his journey from pariah to icon, as he transformed negative attention into a platform for advocacy.

Becoming an Icon

Ultimately, Adin's journey culminated in his recognition as an icon of the LGBTQ movement in Tarvel. His story was no longer one of rejection but of triumph. Adin's advocacy led to significant changes in local policies regarding LGBTQ rights, and he became a sought-after speaker at national conferences. His ability to articulate the struggles and aspirations of the LGBTQ community resonated with a broader audience, solidifying his status as a leader.

$$\text{Icon Status} = \text{Advocacy Impact} + \text{Cultural Relevance} \tag{60}$$

This equation encapsulates the essence of Adin's journey. His icon status was achieved through impactful advocacy and his relevance in the cultural discourse surrounding LGBTQ rights. Adin Xeris emerged not just as a figurehead but as a symbol of hope and resilience for many.

Conclusion

Adin's journey from pariah to icon serves as a powerful reminder of the potential for transformation within individuals and communities. It illustrates the importance of solidarity, resilience, and the ability to turn adversity into advocacy. Adin Xeris's legacy continues to inspire future generations, proving that even in the face of overwhelming opposition, change is possible. His story is not just about one person's fight for equality; it is about the collective struggle for justice, acceptance, and love.

The Aftermath of the Revolution

Adin's Transition into Politics

Adin Xeris's transition into politics was not merely a career change; it was a natural evolution of his lifelong commitment to LGBTQ+ rights and social justice. After years of grassroots activism, Adin recognized that to effectuate real, systemic change, he needed to step into the political arena. This section explores the theories behind political engagement, the challenges faced during this transition, and the examples that illustrate Adin's remarkable journey.

Theoretical Framework

Political engagement can be understood through various theoretical lenses. One pertinent theory is the *Social Movement Theory*, which posits that social movements are critical in shaping political landscapes. According to Tilly and Tarrow (2015), social movements can influence political institutions by creating new political opportunities and altering public perceptions. Adin's activism had already laid the groundwork for a supportive environment, making his transition into politics timely and strategic.

Furthermore, the *Political Opportunity Structure* (POS) theory suggests that the political context in which activists operate can significantly affect their ability to mobilize and influence policy. The POS framework emphasizes the role of political allies, institutional openings, and the broader socio-political climate. Adin's work in Tarvel had garnered attention and support, creating a favorable POS that he could leverage as he sought political office.

Challenges Faced

Transitioning from activism to politics is fraught with challenges. One major obstacle Adin encountered was the skepticism from both the political establishment and some segments of the LGBTQ+ community. Many activists feared that entering politics could compromise their values, leading to a dilution of their advocacy. Adin had to navigate this tension carefully, demonstrating that political engagement could amplify his activism rather than undermine it.

Additionally, the conservative backlash in Tarvel posed a significant threat. Adin's outspoken nature had already drawn ire from traditionalists, and entering politics meant he would be under even greater scrutiny. He faced threats, both online and offline, which tested his resolve. The challenge was not just to advocate for LGBTQ+ rights but to do so in a way that was politically viable and safe.

Strategic Moves

Adin's strategic moves during this transition were crucial to his success. First, he established a strong base of support by forming alliances with other progressive organizations. By collaborating with local environmental groups, women's rights organizations, and labor unions, Adin broadened his appeal and built a coalition that transcended single-issue politics. This coalition-building was essential in a politically polarized environment.

Second, Adin utilized social media effectively to communicate his vision and engage with constituents. He understood that the digital landscape was a powerful tool for political mobilization. His campaign harnessed platforms like Twitter, Instagram, and TikTok to share his message, rally support, and counteract negative narratives. This approach not only resonated with younger voters but also helped humanize his political aspirations.

Examples of Political Engagement

Adin's first foray into politics was marked by his candidacy for the local city council. His campaign was grounded in the principles of inclusivity and representation. He famously stated in a campaign speech, "I'm not just fighting for LGBTQ+ rights; I'm fighting for a Tarvel where everyone can live freely, no matter who they love or how they identify." This resonated deeply with voters who felt marginalized by the existing political landscape.

During his campaign, Adin also focused on key issues that affected the broader community, such as affordable housing, healthcare, and education. By framing LGBTQ+ rights within the context of these universal issues, he was able to attract a diverse voter base. His ability to connect with the electorate on multiple levels exemplified a sophisticated understanding of the intersectionality of social justice.

Impact and Legacy

Adin's transition into politics ultimately reshaped the political landscape of Tarvel. His election to the city council marked a significant milestone for LGBTQ+ representation in local government. He championed initiatives that directly benefited the LGBTQ+ community, such as anti-discrimination ordinances and funding for LGBTQ+ youth programs.

Moreover, Adin's political journey inspired a new generation of activists to consider political engagement as a viable path for change. His story became a rallying cry for many who previously felt disillusioned with the political process. As he once said, "Activism doesn't stop at the protest; it continues in the halls of power."

In conclusion, Adin Xeris's transition into politics illustrates the complex interplay between activism and political engagement. His journey underscores the importance of strategic alliances, effective communication, and the courage to confront challenges head-on. Adin not only carved a path for himself but also opened doors for future activists seeking to make a difference in their communities.

Continuing the Fight on a Global Scale

In the wake of Adin Xeris's monumental achievements in Tarvel, the fight for LGBTQ+ rights transitioned from a localized struggle to a global movement. Adin's legacy served as a beacon of hope and inspiration, igniting passion in activists around the world. This section explores the theoretical frameworks, ongoing challenges, and notable examples of how the fight for LGBTQ+ rights has expanded beyond national borders.

Theoretical Frameworks

To understand the global LGBTQ+ rights movement, it is essential to consider various theoretical frameworks that underpin activism. One such framework is **Intersectionality**, coined by Kimberlé Crenshaw, which posits that individuals experience oppression in varying configurations and degrees of intensity based on overlapping social identities. This is crucial for LGBTQ+ activists as they navigate the complexities of race, gender, and sexual orientation. Adin's work exemplified intersectionality by advocating for marginalized voices within the LGBTQ+ community, ensuring that the fight for equality was inclusive.

Another important theory is **Postcolonial Theory**, which examines the impact of colonial histories on contemporary social structures. Many LGBTQ+ activists in formerly colonized nations face unique challenges, as colonial laws and cultural legacies often criminalize same-sex relationships. Understanding these historical contexts is vital for crafting effective advocacy strategies that resonate with diverse communities.

Ongoing Challenges

Despite significant progress, the global LGBTQ+ rights movement faces numerous challenges. One major issue is the **Criminalization of Homosexuality**, which persists in many countries. As of 2023, approximately 70 countries still have laws that criminalize same-sex relationships, often resulting in severe penalties, including imprisonment and violence. Activists must navigate these hostile environments while advocating for change.

Another pressing challenge is **Cultural Resistance**. In many societies, deeply entrenched cultural norms and religious beliefs oppose LGBTQ+ rights. For instance, in parts of Africa and the Middle East, traditional values often clash with the push for equality, leading to backlash against activists. The fight for LGBTQ+ rights must be sensitive to these cultural dynamics while promoting universal human rights.

Notable Examples of Global Activism

Adin's influence extended beyond Tarvel, inspiring activists worldwide to adopt innovative strategies for advocacy. One notable example is the **Global Pride Movement**, which unites LGBTQ+ individuals across borders to celebrate diversity and demand rights. Events such as World Pride and International Day Against Homophobia, Transphobia, and Biphobia (IDAHOTB) have become platforms for raising awareness and mobilizing support.

In addition, grassroots organizations like **OutRight Action International** work tirelessly to document human rights abuses against LGBTQ+ individuals globally. Their reports highlight the dire situations faced by LGBTQ+ people in oppressive regimes, urging international bodies to take action. Adin's advocacy for LGBTQ+ rights in Tarvel parallels these efforts, as he emphasized the importance of documenting and publicizing injustices.

Collaborative Efforts and Alliances

Continuing the fight on a global scale requires collaboration among diverse organizations and movements. One successful model is the formation of **Coalitions**, where LGBTQ+ groups partner with women's rights, racial justice, and humanitarian organizations. For instance, the **Coalition for Global Equality** brings together various stakeholders to advocate for comprehensive LGBTQ+ rights legislation at the United Nations.

Moreover, social media has emerged as a powerful tool for global activism. Campaigns like **#LoveIsLove** and **#Pride2023** have transcended borders, allowing individuals to share their stories and connect with others facing similar struggles. Adin's use of social media to amplify voices in Tarvel serves as a precursor to these global movements, demonstrating the effectiveness of digital platforms in fostering solidarity.

Conclusion

Adin Xeris's legacy is not merely a local phenomenon; it has catalyzed a global movement for LGBTQ+ rights. By employing intersectional approaches, addressing ongoing challenges, and fostering collaborative efforts, activists worldwide continue to build on the foundation laid by pioneers like Adin. The fight for equality is far from over, but with each passing day, the collective strength of the global LGBTQ+ community grows, pushing the boundaries of what is possible.

As we reflect on the ongoing battle for LGBTQ+ rights, it is crucial to remember that every voice matters, and every action counts. Adin's journey from a closeted individual in Tarvel to a global icon serves as a powerful reminder that change is possible, and together, we can continue the fight for justice and equality for all.

The establishment of Adin's advocacy foundation

In the wake of significant victories for LGBTQ rights in Tarvel, Adin Xeris recognized the necessity of creating a structured and sustainable platform for advocacy. Thus, the establishment of the Adin Xeris Advocacy Foundation (AXAF) marked a pivotal moment not only in Adin's life but also in the ongoing struggle for equality. The foundation aimed to address various issues facing the LGBTQ community, including legal rights, mental health resources, and educational outreach.

The Foundation's Mission and Vision

The mission of AXAF was clear: to empower LGBTQ individuals, advocate for equitable laws, and foster a culture of acceptance. Adin envisioned a world where everyone, regardless of sexual orientation or gender identity, could live authentically without fear of discrimination. The foundation's vision was rooted in the belief that advocacy should not only focus on immediate legal changes but also promote long-term societal transformation.

Key Areas of Focus

To fulfill its mission, AXAF identified several key areas of focus:

- **Legal Advocacy:** The foundation aimed to support legal battles for LGBTQ rights, including anti-discrimination laws and marriage equality. This involved collaborating with legal experts and other advocacy groups to challenge unjust legislation.

- **Mental Health Support:** Recognizing the high rates of mental health issues within the LGBTQ community, AXAF prioritized the establishment of support networks and resources. This included funding for therapy programs and creating safe spaces for individuals to discuss their experiences.

- **Educational Outreach:** The foundation sought to educate both the LGBTQ community and the general public about issues related to sexual orientation and gender identity. This involved developing educational materials, hosting workshops, and partnering with schools to implement inclusive curricula.

- **Youth Empowerment:** AXAF placed a strong emphasis on empowering LGBTQ youth. This included mentorship programs, scholarships for LGBTQ students, and initiatives to combat bullying in schools.

THE AFTERMATH OF THE REVOLUTION

Challenges in Establishing the Foundation

Despite the enthusiasm surrounding the establishment of AXAF, Adin faced numerous challenges. One significant hurdle was securing funding. While initial donations from supporters provided a foundation, sustaining financial resources required strategic planning and outreach. Adin organized fundraising events, including benefit concerts and auctions, to garner support.

Additionally, the foundation faced opposition from conservative groups who viewed AXAF as a threat to traditional values. This opposition manifested in public protests and negative media campaigns. In response, Adin utilized his platform to advocate for the foundation's mission, emphasizing the importance of inclusivity and understanding.

The Impact of AXAF

The establishment of AXAF had a profound impact on the LGBTQ community in Tarvel and beyond. Within the first year, the foundation successfully lobbied for the passage of local anti-discrimination laws, providing a legal framework that protected LGBTQ individuals from workplace and housing discrimination.

Moreover, the mental health initiatives launched by AXAF significantly reduced barriers to accessing mental health services. By partnering with local therapists and counselors, the foundation facilitated support groups that became lifelines for many individuals grappling with their identities.

The educational outreach programs led to increased awareness and understanding of LGBTQ issues in Tarvel schools. As a result, students reported feeling safer and more accepted, leading to a decline in bullying incidents.

Conclusion

The establishment of the Adin Xeris Advocacy Foundation was not merely a personal achievement for Adin but a transformative step towards achieving broader societal change. Through its focus on legal advocacy, mental health, education, and youth empowerment, AXAF became a beacon of hope for the LGBTQ community, demonstrating that organized efforts could lead to tangible progress. As Adin often stated, "Change starts with us, but it requires a collective effort to sustain it." The foundation's ongoing work continues to inspire future generations of activists and advocates, ensuring that Adin's legacy lives on in the fight for equality.

Adin's memoirs and the documentary on their life

Adin Xeris' journey from a closeted individual in the conservative town of Tarvel to a celebrated LGBTQ activist is a narrative that transcends mere biography; it is a testament to the power of resilience, community, and the relentless pursuit of equality. The release of Adin's memoirs, titled *Unapologetically Me: The Journey of Adin Xeris*, coincided with the premiere of the documentary *Fighting for Love: The Adin Xeris Story*. Together, these works serve not only as a chronicle of Adin's life but also as a cultural artifact that captures the zeitgeist of a transformative era in LGBTQ rights.

The Memoirs: A Deep Dive into Adin's Life

Adin's memoirs provide an intimate glimpse into the struggles and triumphs that shaped their identity. The narrative is structured chronologically, beginning with Adin's childhood in Tarvel, where conservative values dictated social norms. Adin writes candidly about the pressure to conform and the fear of being different, encapsulating the internal conflict faced by many in the LGBTQ community. For example, in one poignant chapter, Adin recalls a pivotal moment during high school when they were confronted by peers about their sexuality. The visceral emotions depicted in passages such as:

> "I felt like a ghost, haunting the hallways of my own life, invisible to those who claimed to know me. But inside, I was screaming, 'This is not who I am!'"

highlight the profound isolation experienced by LGBTQ youth.

The memoir also explores the role of friendship and acceptance in Adin's life. The transformative power of a single friend's acceptance is illustrated through anecdotes that reveal how this support became a catalyst for Adin's activism. The memoir culminates in a call to action, urging readers to embrace their authentic selves and fight against societal oppression.

The Documentary: A Visual Representation of Activism

Complementing the memoirs, the documentary *Fighting for Love* employs a mix of archival footage, interviews, and reenactments to depict Adin's life story. Directed by acclaimed filmmaker Jamie Lee, the documentary captures the essence of Adin's activism, showcasing pivotal moments such as the first LGBTQ awareness march in Tarvel.

One of the documentary's strengths lies in its ability to juxtapose personal narrative with broader societal issues. For instance, scenes of Adin speaking at national conferences are interspersed with footage of protests and legislative battles, effectively illustrating the connection between personal struggle and collective action. The documentary features interviews with prominent LGBTQ activists, who reflect on Adin's impact on the movement, stating:

> "Adin didn't just fight for their rights; they fought for all of us. They made it clear that our stories matter."

This sentiment encapsulates the documentary's overarching theme: the interconnectedness of individual and collective struggles within the LGBTQ rights movement.

Theoretical Implications and Cultural Impact

The release of Adin's memoirs and the documentary coincides with a critical moment in LGBTQ discourse, where personal narratives are increasingly recognized as vital to understanding the complexities of identity and activism. Drawing on the theories of intersectionality posited by scholars such as Kimberlé Crenshaw, Adin's story exemplifies how various aspects of identity—sexual orientation, race, and socio-economic status—interact to shape experiences of oppression and resistance.

Moreover, the memoir and documentary serve as educational tools, fostering empathy and understanding among audiences. They challenge viewers to confront their biases and consider the broader implications of LGBTQ rights. For example, the documentary features a segment on the backlash faced by Adin during their fight for marriage equality, highlighting the societal tensions that often accompany progressive movements.

Conclusion: A Lasting Legacy

Adin's memoirs and the documentary not only document a significant life but also contribute to the ongoing dialogue surrounding LGBTQ rights. They provide a platform for future generations to learn from the past while inspiring them to continue the fight for equality. As Adin poignantly states in the closing lines of the memoir:

> "We are the authors of our stories, and together, we will write a future where love knows no bounds."

This powerful message reinforces the idea that while Adin's personal journey may have reached a conclusion, the legacy of their activism will continue to inspire and empower countless others in the quest for justice and acceptance.

Adin's Final Battle

Adin's Final Battle

Adin's Final Battle

In the twilight of his activism, Adin Xeris faced the most formidable opponent of his life: a health challenge that would test not only his physical resilience but also the strength of the community he had fought so hard to uplift. This chapter delves into the trials of Adin's unexpected diagnosis, the unwavering support he received from his community, and his last public address, which would resonate through the halls of activism for years to come.

Section 1: Health Challenges and Resilience

Subsection 1: Adin's Unexpected Diagnosis Adin's life took a dramatic turn when he received a diagnosis that shook him to his core. It was a moment that felt surreal, as if the universe had conspired to throw him into the depths of a personal battle just as he was emerging victorious in his public crusade. The diagnosis was serious, and Adin was faced with the harsh realities of illness, a stark contrast to the vibrant life he had carved out as an activist.

This unexpected twist forced Adin to confront his mortality. The psychological impact of such a diagnosis can be profound, often leading to what medical professionals refer to as the "existential crisis." It is a moment when one grapples with the meaning of life, the legacy they will leave behind, and the unfinished business that lingers. Adin found himself in this space, questioning everything he had fought for and whether he would have the chance to see it through.

Subsection 2: The Power of Community and Support During Illness In times of crisis, the strength of community is often revealed. For Adin, this was a moment of profound realization. The LGBTQ community he had fought to empower rallied around him, providing not just emotional support but also practical assistance. Friends and allies organized fundraisers to cover medical expenses, while others created a network of care that ensured Adin was never alone during his treatment.

The concept of "chosen family" within the LGBTQ community is a powerful testament to resilience. Adin experienced firsthand the ways in which community can act as a buffer against the isolating effects of illness. This support system mirrored the very essence of activism—collective action and solidarity. As Adin navigated his treatment, he found solace in the fact that he was not just a solitary figure fighting for rights; he was part of a larger tapestry of love and support.

Subsection 3: Adin's Last Public Address Standing Strong Despite the challenges he faced, Adin was determined to make one last public address. This moment was not just about him; it was about the movement, the people who had stood by him, and the future of LGBTQ rights. He took to the stage with a vigor that belied his condition, speaking to an audience filled with supporters who had been inspired by his journey.

In his address, Adin articulated the core tenets of his activism, emphasizing the importance of resilience and the ongoing fight for equality. He reminded everyone that activism is not just about the victories; it's also about the struggles and the solidarity that emerges from them. Adin's words were laced with a sense of urgency, urging the next generation of activists to continue the fight, to not let the flame of equality dim in the face of adversity.

$$\text{Activism} = \text{Resilience} + \text{Community Support} + \text{Legacy} \qquad (61)$$

This equation encapsulates Adin's philosophy, suggesting that true activism is a product of resilience bolstered by community support, all while being mindful of the legacy one leaves behind.

As he concluded his speech, the audience erupted in applause, a standing ovation that felt like a collective heartbeat of gratitude and admiration. Adin, standing strong despite the weight of his diagnosis, became a symbol of courage and perseverance.

Conclusion Adin's final battle was not merely a personal struggle; it was a reflection of the broader fight for LGBTQ rights. His journey illuminated the intersection of health, identity, and activism, showcasing the resilience of both the individual and the community. The lessons learned from this chapter extend beyond Adin's life, serving as a reminder that the fight for equality is ongoing and that every voice matters in the chorus of change.

In the face of adversity, Adin Xeris emerged not just as an activist but as a beacon of hope, a testament to the power of community, and a reminder that even in our darkest moments, we can find strength and purpose. His legacy would continue to inspire generations, proving that battles may be fought on many fronts, but the spirit of activism is indomitable.

Health Challenges and Resilience

Adin's unexpected diagnosis

In the midst of his rising activism, Adin Xeris faced an unexpected challenge that would test his resilience and determination. At the peak of his efforts to advocate for LGBTQ rights in Tarvel, he received a diagnosis that would change the course of his life: he was diagnosed with an autoimmune disease, a condition that not only threatened his physical health but also posed significant emotional and psychological challenges.

The Diagnosis

The diagnosis came during a routine check-up. Adin had been feeling unusually fatigued, experiencing joint pain, and suffering from unexplained weight loss. These symptoms, often dismissed as stress-related side effects of his activism, were finally brought to light when his doctor, after a series of tests, revealed that Adin had *Systemic Lupus Erythematosus* (SLE). This autoimmune disease occurs when the body's immune system mistakenly attacks healthy tissue, leading to inflammation and damage in various organs.

$$\text{SLE} = \sum_{i=1}^{n} (\text{Immune response})_i - (\text{Healthy tissue})_i \tag{62}$$

The implications of this diagnosis were profound. Adin was not just facing a chronic illness; he was also confronted with the reality of needing to manage his health while continuing his advocacy work. The emotional toll of the diagnosis was compounded by the fear of how it might affect his public persona and the perception of his capabilities as an activist.

Emotional and Psychological Impact

Adin's initial reaction to the diagnosis was one of disbelief followed by a profound sense of vulnerability. He had always been the strong, vocal leader in the LGBTQ community, and now he found himself grappling with feelings of inadequacy and fear. The very essence of his identity as an activist seemed to be at odds with his new reality as a patient.

The psychological implications of living with a chronic illness can be extensive. Studies have shown that individuals diagnosed with autoimmune diseases often experience higher rates of anxiety and depression. Adin was no exception. He found himself questioning his worth and the sustainability of his activism.

$$\text{Mental Health} = f(\text{Chronic Illness, Social Support, Coping Mechanisms}) \quad (63)$$

Where: - f represents a function that describes the relationship between mental health and various factors. - Chronic Illness refers to the diagnosis of SLE. - Social Support includes the encouragement from friends, family, and the LGBTQ community. - Coping Mechanisms involve strategies Adin employed to manage stress and anxiety.

Adin's friends and fellow activists rallied around him, providing a support network that was crucial in navigating this new chapter of his life. However, the stigma surrounding chronic illness, particularly in the context of activism, loomed large. Adin feared that his diagnosis might be perceived as a weakness, undermining the credibility he had built as a leader.

Finding Strength in Vulnerability

Despite the initial turmoil, Adin began to realize that his diagnosis could serve as a powerful tool for advocacy. By sharing his journey with SLE, he could highlight the importance of mental health awareness and the need for support systems for those battling chronic illnesses.

Adin's experience resonated with many in the LGBTQ community, who often face their own struggles with health and acceptance. He began to speak openly about his diagnosis at events, emphasizing the need for compassion and understanding.

$$\text{Advocacy} = \text{Awareness} + \text{Empathy} + \text{Action} \quad (64)$$

This equation illustrates how Adin leveraged his personal experience to foster a greater understanding of the intersection between health and identity. By advocating for mental health resources and support for those with chronic illnesses, Adin not only reclaimed his narrative but also empowered others to do the same.

Conclusion

Adin's unexpected diagnosis was a pivotal moment in his life, forcing him to confront his vulnerabilities while also providing an opportunity to expand his advocacy efforts. Through resilience and the support of his community, he transformed a personal battle into a broader movement for awareness and acceptance, reinforcing the idea that strength can be found in vulnerability. As he continued to fight for LGBTQ rights, Adin also championed the cause of those living with chronic illnesses, ensuring that their voices were heard and their experiences validated.

In the end, Adin's journey through illness not only shaped his activism but also left an indelible mark on the LGBTQ community, inspiring countless individuals to embrace their struggles and advocate for change.

The power of community and support during illness

In the tumultuous journey of life, illness can often feel like a solitary battle. However, as Adin Xeris faced unexpected health challenges, it became abundantly clear that the power of community and support can transform the experience from one of isolation to one of solidarity and strength. This section delves into the profound impact that community support has on individuals grappling with health issues, particularly within the LGBTQ+ context.

The Importance of Community Support

The LGBTQ+ community has historically been a source of resilience and empowerment. For many individuals, especially those like Adin who have spent years advocating for equality, the community serves as a chosen family—a network of support that understands the unique struggles faced by its members. Research indicates that social support can significantly affect health outcomes, providing emotional, informational, and practical assistance during times of crisis.

$$S = E + I + P \tag{65}$$

Where S represents social support, E is emotional support, I is informational support, and P is practical support. This equation illustrates the multifaceted nature of community support, where each component plays a crucial role in enhancing an individual's coping mechanisms during illness.

Emotional Support: A Pillar of Strength

Adin's diagnosis was met with an outpouring of emotional support from friends, family, and fellow activists. Emotional support involves expressions of empathy, love, trust, and caring, which can alleviate feelings of loneliness and despair. For instance, during Adin's treatment, a group of local LGBTQ+ activists organized a weekly gathering where they shared stories, offered encouragement, and celebrated small victories together. This initiative not only bolstered Adin's spirits but also fostered a sense of belonging, reminding him that he was not alone in his fight.

Informational Support: Knowledge is Power

In addition to emotional backing, informational support proved vital. Friends and community members shared resources about treatment options, coping strategies, and mental health support. This sharing of knowledge can be encapsulated in the following equation:

$$K = R + E \tag{66}$$

Where K is knowledge, R represents resources shared, and E is experience-based insights. For Adin, this meant not just receiving information about medical procedures but also learning from others who had faced similar battles. This community exchange of knowledge empowered him to make informed decisions about his health and treatment.

Practical Support: Actions Speak Louder Than Words

Practical support encompasses tangible assistance, such as help with daily tasks, transportation to medical appointments, or even financial aid. During his illness, Adin received an overwhelming amount of practical support from his community. Activists organized fundraising events, ensuring that Adin could focus on his recovery without the added stress of financial burdens. This collective action is a testament to the adage that "it takes a village."

For example, a local bake sale organized by community members raised over $10,000, demonstrating that practical support can manifest in creative and impactful ways. This not only alleviated financial pressures but also reinforced the idea that the community was actively engaged in Adin's journey, standing by him in a time of need.

The Role of LGBTQ+ Community in Mental Health

The LGBTQ+ community has long been an advocate for mental health awareness, recognizing that the intersection of identity and health can lead to unique challenges. Adin's experience during his illness highlighted the importance of mental health support within the community.

Studies suggest that individuals who identify as LGBTQ+ often face higher rates of anxiety and depression due to societal stigma and discrimination. The presence of a supportive community can mitigate these effects, fostering resilience and encouraging individuals to seek help when needed.

Adin's friends initiated a mental health support group specifically for LGBTQ+ individuals dealing with illness, creating a safe space for sharing experiences and coping strategies. This group not only provided emotional support but also encouraged members to seek professional help, thereby promoting a holistic approach to health that encompasses both physical and mental well-being.

Conclusion: The Lasting Impact of Community Support

As Adin navigated the challenges of his illness, the power of community support became a cornerstone of his resilience. The emotional, informational, and practical assistance provided by his friends and fellow activists not only aided in his recovery but also reinforced the bonds within the LGBTQ+ community.

This experience serves as a powerful reminder that in times of crisis, the strength of community can be a formidable ally. Adin Xeris's journey illustrates that while illness may test our limits, it can also illuminate the profound connections we share with others. The legacy of support and solidarity established during this time continues to inspire others, emphasizing that together, we are stronger.

In the end, Adin's story is not just about overcoming illness; it is a celebration of community, love, and the unwavering spirit of those who stand together in the face of adversity. The lessons learned from his experience resonate far beyond his personal journey, reminding us all of the importance of nurturing our communities and supporting one another through life's trials.

Adin's last public address standing strong

In the twilight of Adin Xeris' remarkable journey, the last public address he delivered became a powerful testament to his resilience and unwavering commitment to the LGBTQ+ community. This moment was not merely a speech;

it was a culmination of years of struggle, triumph, and the relentless fight for equality in Tarvel and beyond.

Context of the Address

The atmosphere was charged with emotion as Adin stood before a crowd that had gathered to honor his legacy. This was not just another rally; it was a pivotal moment in the ongoing struggle for LGBTQ+ rights. The community had faced numerous challenges, from local legislative hurdles to societal prejudice, and Adin's address was a clarion call for unity and perseverance.

Key Themes of the Address

Adin's address focused on several key themes that resonated deeply with his audience:

- **Resilience in Adversity:** Adin spoke candidly about the health challenges he faced, emphasizing the importance of resilience. He quoted, "We are not defined by our struggles but by how we rise from them." This sentiment was a reminder that adversity could be transformed into strength.

- **The Power of Community:** He highlighted the role of the LGBTQ+ community in providing support during difficult times. Adin stated, "Together, we are an unstoppable force. When one of us falls, we all lift them up." This message reinforced the idea that solidarity is essential in the fight for equality.

- **The Ongoing Fight for Rights:** Adin urged the audience not to become complacent. "Our rights are not a gift; they are a fight," he declared. This call to action served as a reminder that vigilance is necessary to protect the hard-won rights of the LGBTQ+ community.

- **Hope for Future Generations:** He expressed his hope for a future where love and acceptance would reign supreme. "We owe it to the next generation to continue this fight," he said, inspiring the youth present to carry the torch of activism forward.

Theoretical Framework

The impact of Adin's speech can be analyzed through the lens of social movement theory, particularly the concept of collective identity. According to Tilly and Tarrow

(2015), collective identity plays a crucial role in mobilizing individuals within social movements. Adin's address served to reinforce a shared identity among LGBTQ+ individuals and allies, fostering a sense of belonging and purpose.

Furthermore, the theory of emotional resonance posits that speeches that evoke strong emotions can lead to increased engagement and activism (Meyer, 2002). Adin's poignant recounting of personal struggles and triumphs not only resonated emotionally but also galvanized the audience to take action.

Examples and Impact

In his address, Adin shared personal anecdotes that illustrated the challenges faced by LGBTQ+ individuals in Tarvel. For instance, he recounted a story about a young activist who faced severe backlash from their family but found solace in the community. This narrative exemplified the real-world implications of societal prejudice and the importance of community support.

The impact of Adin's final address was immediate and profound. Following the speech, there was a noticeable surge in community engagement, with many individuals expressing their desire to become more involved in activism. Social media platforms erupted with hashtags like `#StandWithAdin` and `#FightForEquality`, creating a virtual movement that extended beyond the confines of Tarvel.

Conclusion

Adin Xeris' last public address was not merely a farewell; it was a rallying cry for the future of LGBTQ+ rights. Through themes of resilience, community, and hope, Adin left an indelible mark on the hearts of those who gathered to hear him speak. His legacy would continue to inspire generations of activists, reminding them that the fight for equality is ongoing and that every voice matters.

As the crowd dispersed, many carried with them the weight of Adin's words, ready to take up the mantle of activism and continue the fight for a world where love knows no boundaries. Adin Xeris may have left the stage, but his spirit and message would live on, echoing in the hearts of those who dare to dream of a more inclusive future.

A Farewell to a Revolutionary

Adin's Lasting Impact on Tarvel and Beyond

Adin Xeris, a name that resonates with the echoes of change, left an indelible mark on Tarvel and the broader LGBTQ+ movement. His journey from a closeted individual to a pioneering activist exemplifies the transformative power of advocacy, and his legacy continues to inspire generations.

Changing Social Norms

Adin's activism catalyzed a shift in social norms within Tarvel, a town that had long been steeped in conservative values. Before Adin's emergence, discussions surrounding LGBTQ+ rights were often hushed, relegated to whispers in dark corners. However, through his fearless approach, Adin challenged the status quo. He utilized humor and charisma, reminiscent of the comedic style of Dave Chappelle, to engage audiences that might otherwise have remained indifferent.

$$\text{Social Change} = \text{Awareness} + \text{Advocacy} \tag{67}$$

Where: - **Awareness** refers to the understanding and acknowledgment of LGBTQ+ issues. - **Advocacy** involves active support and promotion of LGBTQ+ rights.

Adin's ability to blend humor with hard-hitting truths allowed him to reach diverse audiences, fostering a culture of acceptance and understanding. His public speeches often included anecdotes that highlighted the absurdity of discrimination, drawing laughter while simultaneously provoking thought.

Empowerment of Local LGBTQ+ Community

The formation of local LGBTQ+ groups under Adin's leadership was pivotal. He organized events that not only celebrated identity but also provided safe spaces for individuals to express themselves freely. For instance, the inaugural LGBTQ+ Awareness March in Tarvel, spearheaded by Adin, attracted a record number of participants, showcasing solidarity and community spirit.

$$\text{Community Engagement} = \text{Participation} \times \text{Visibility} \tag{68}$$

Where: - **Participation** is the involvement of community members in LGBTQ+ events. - **Visibility** refers to the public acknowledgment and representation of LGBTQ+ individuals.

The march served as a turning point, demonstrating to both supporters and opponents that the LGBTQ+ community in Tarvel was not only present but also united. Adin's ability to galvanize support was instrumental in transforming Tarvel into a more inclusive environment.

Legal and Political Influence

Adin's activism also had significant legal implications. His relentless lobbying efforts contributed to the repeal of discriminatory laws in Tarvel, paving the way for marriage equality. The landmark Supreme Court case that Adin championed became a reference point for similar movements across the country.

$$\text{Legal Change} = \text{Advocacy} + \text{Judicial Support} \tag{69}$$

Where: - **Judicial Support** reflects the backing of the judiciary in recognizing and upholding LGBTQ+ rights.

Adin's legal battles not only transformed Tarvel but also set a precedent for other regions grappling with similar issues, demonstrating that grassroots activism could lead to significant legislative change.

Cultural Impact and Representation

Beyond legal frameworks, Adin's influence permeated the cultural fabric of Tarvel. He became a symbol of resilience and hope, inspiring artists, writers, and performers to explore LGBTQ+ themes in their work. The annual celebrations of Adin's birthday evolved into a cultural festival that highlighted LGBTQ+ art, music, and history, ensuring that the narratives of marginalized voices were amplified.

$$\text{Cultural Legacy} = \text{Representation} + \text{Education} \tag{70}$$

Where: - **Representation** refers to the inclusion of LGBTQ+ stories and figures in mainstream culture. - **Education** encompasses initiatives aimed at informing the public about LGBTQ+ history and rights.

Adin's story became a source of inspiration for countless individuals, encouraging them to embrace their identities and advocate for their rights.

Global Influence

Adin's impact transcended the borders of Tarvel, influencing LGBTQ+ movements globally. His advocacy model became a blueprint for activists in other conservative regions, demonstrating that change was possible through community organizing and strategic engagement.

$$\text{Global Activism} = \text{Local Success} \times \text{Network Expansion} \qquad (71)$$

Where: - **Local Success** refers to the achievements of LGBTQ+ movements in specific areas. - **Network Expansion** involves the growth of connections among activists worldwide.

Through social media, Adin's message reached international audiences, fostering a sense of global solidarity among LGBTQ+ individuals. His legacy is a testament to the power of one voice to inspire collective action across the world.

In conclusion, Adin Xeris' lasting impact on Tarvel and beyond is a multifaceted legacy characterized by social change, community empowerment, legal victories, cultural representation, and global influence. His journey serves as a reminder that the fight for equality is ongoing, and each individual's contribution is vital in the quest for justice and acceptance.

Honoring Adin's memory and legacy as an activist

The legacy of Adin Xeris transcends the confines of Tarvel and resonates within the broader narrative of LGBTQ+ rights advocacy. To honor Adin's memory is not merely to remember a person; it is to celebrate the collective struggle for equality and to perpetuate the ideals for which Adin fought tirelessly. This section explores the various ways in which Adin's legacy is honored, the challenges faced in the commemoration of activists, and the theoretical frameworks that guide such memorialization.

Theoretical Frameworks for Memorialization

The act of memorializing an activist like Adin can be understood through several theoretical lenses. One significant framework is the *Collective Memory Theory*, which posits that communities remember their past through shared narratives that shape their identity and values. According to Halbwachs (1992), collective memory is constructed through social interactions and cultural practices. In the case of Adin, the LGBTQ+ community in Tarvel and beyond constructs a narrative that not only honors Adin's contributions but also reinforces a collective identity rooted in resilience and activism.

$$M = \frac{C + I + P}{T} \qquad (72)$$

Where:

+ M = Memory of the activist

+ C = Community narratives

+ I = Individual stories of impact

+ P = Public commemorations

+ T = Time elapsed since the activism

This equation illustrates that the memory of Adin is a function of community narratives, individual stories, public commemorations, and the time elapsed since their activism. As time progresses, the weight of Adin's contributions becomes more pronounced, necessitating ongoing efforts to honor their legacy.

Public Commemorations and Events

One of the most significant ways to honor Adin's memory is through public commemorations. These events serve as a platform for reflection, education, and mobilization. For instance, the annual *Adin Xeris Memorial March* has become a cornerstone event in Tarvel, drawing participants from diverse backgrounds to celebrate Adin's life and contributions. During this march, speeches from fellow activists and community leaders highlight the ongoing struggles faced by the LGBTQ+ community, reminding participants of the work that remains unfinished.

Moreover, the establishment of the *Adin Xeris Foundation* plays a crucial role in perpetuating Adin's legacy. The foundation focuses on education, advocacy, and support for LGBTQ+ youth, embodying Adin's commitment to uplifting marginalized voices. The foundation's initiatives include scholarships for LGBTQ+ students, workshops on activism, and funding for community projects that align with Adin's vision of equality.

Challenges in Commemoration

While honoring Adin's memory is essential, it is not without challenges. One significant issue is the potential for *Co-optation*, where the essence of Adin's activism may be diluted or misrepresented by commercial interests or political agendas. This phenomenon often occurs during pride celebrations or other events that may exploit the legacy of activists for profit, overshadowing the original message of equality and justice.

Additionally, there is the challenge of ensuring that the commemoration remains inclusive and representative of the diverse experiences within the LGBTQ+ community. As Adin was a proponent of intersectionality, it is crucial that their legacy honors not only the struggles of those who identify as LGBTQ+ but also those who face compounded discrimination based on race, gender, and socioeconomic status.

Inspiring Future Generations

Honoring Adin's memory also entails a commitment to inspiring future generations of activists. Educational programs that share Adin's story and the history of LGBTQ+ rights are vital in fostering a sense of agency among young individuals. These programs can include workshops, lectures, and mentorship opportunities that encourage youth to engage in activism and understand the historical context of their rights.

Furthermore, art and culture play a significant role in memorializing Adin's legacy. The creation of murals, literature, and performances that reflect Adin's journey can serve as powerful tools for education and inspiration. For example, the *Adin Xeris Art Collective* showcases works that explore themes of identity, resistance, and love, ensuring that Adin's spirit continues to inspire creativity and activism.

Conclusion

In conclusion, honoring Adin Xeris' memory as an activist is a multifaceted endeavor that requires a commitment to collective memory, public commemoration, and the inspiration of future generations. By utilizing theoretical frameworks that guide memorialization, addressing the challenges of co-optation and inclusivity, and fostering a culture of activism through education and the arts, the legacy of Adin Xeris can endure as a beacon of hope and a call to action for all who seek to continue the fight for LGBTQ+ rights. As we reflect on Adin's life, we are reminded that their legacy is not just a memory; it is a movement that lives on in the hearts and actions of those who dare to dream of a more equitable world.

Adin Xeris: The Legend Lives On

Adin's influence on pop culture and art

Adin Xeris emerged as a pivotal figure in the realm of LGBTQ activism, but his influence transcended mere advocacy; it seeped deeply into the fabric of pop culture and art. In a world where representation is paramount, Adin's journey resonated with countless individuals, inspiring a wave of creativity that celebrated diversity and challenged societal norms.

Theoretical Framework

To understand Adin's impact, we can draw upon several theoretical frameworks, including cultural studies and queer theory. Cultural studies emphasize the role of media and art in shaping societal values and identities. According to Stuart Hall's encoding/decoding model, media texts are not just passively consumed; they are actively interpreted by audiences based on their own experiences and cultural contexts. This model is crucial when analyzing how Adin's story was received and reinterpreted in various artistic expressions.

Queer theory, on the other hand, challenges the binary understanding of gender and sexuality, advocating for fluidity and inclusivity. Judith Butler's concept of gender performativity suggests that gender is not an innate quality but rather a series of actions and expressions that can be subverted. Adin's visibility and activism prompted artists to explore and express these themes, leading to a richer, more nuanced portrayal of LGBTQ identities in pop culture.

Artistic Expressions Inspired by Adin

Adin's activism inspired a myriad of artistic expressions, from visual arts to performance. One of the most notable examples is the emergence of street art and murals celebrating LGBTQ pride in Tarvel and beyond. Artists began to use public spaces as canvases to convey messages of love, acceptance, and resistance. These works often featured vibrant colors and bold statements, echoing Adin's own passionate calls for equality.

For instance, a mural in downtown Tarvel depicted Adin alongside historical LGBTQ figures, symbolizing the continuity of the struggle for rights. This mural not only honored Adin's contributions but also served as a reminder of the ongoing fight for equality. The artwork became a gathering place for community members, fostering a sense of solidarity and shared purpose.

Pop Culture References

Adin's influence also permeated mainstream media. His story was adapted into a critically acclaimed documentary titled *Fighting for Freedom: The Adin Xeris Story*, which chronicled his journey from a closeted youth to a leading activist. The film not only highlighted his achievements but also showcased the personal struggles he faced, making it relatable to a wide audience. Critics praised the documentary for its honest portrayal of the complexities of identity and activism, reinforcing the idea that personal narratives are powerful tools for social change.

In addition, Adin became a sought-after figure in the world of fashion. Designers began to incorporate LGBTQ themes into their collections, celebrating diversity on the runway. Adin's appearances at fashion shows, often donning outfits that challenged traditional gender norms, made headlines and sparked conversations about the intersection of fashion and identity. This phenomenon illustrates how pop culture can be a vehicle for activism, with Adin at the forefront of this movement.

Challenges and Critiques

Despite the positive impact of Adin's influence on pop culture, it is essential to acknowledge the challenges and critiques that arose. Some critics argued that the commercialization of LGBTQ themes in art and media risked diluting the original messages of activism. The commodification of identity can lead to a superficial understanding of the struggles faced by LGBTQ individuals, reducing complex issues to mere trends.

Moreover, there was a concern that the focus on prominent figures like Adin could overshadow the voices of marginalized communities within the LGBTQ spectrum. It is crucial to recognize that while Adin's story is significant, it is just one of many narratives that deserve attention. The challenge lies in ensuring that the broader spectrum of LGBTQ experiences is represented in pop culture, avoiding a singular narrative that may perpetuate stereotypes.

Conclusion

In conclusion, Adin Xeris' influence on pop culture and art is a testament to the power of activism in shaping societal narratives. Through various artistic expressions, Adin's journey has inspired a generation of creators to explore themes of identity, acceptance, and resistance. While challenges remain, the ongoing dialogue sparked by Adin's legacy continues to push the boundaries of representation in the arts. As we celebrate his contributions, it is essential to remain vigilant in amplifying diverse voices within the LGBTQ community, ensuring that the fight for equality is both inclusive and transformative.

Celebrating Adin's achievements annually

In the vibrant town of Tarvel, the annual celebration of Adin Xeris' achievements has become a cornerstone of the LGBTQ+ community's calendar. This event not only honors Adin's legacy but also serves as a rallying point for ongoing advocacy and education in the fight for equality. Each year, the celebration takes on a unique theme, reflecting the evolving challenges and victories faced by the LGBTQ+ movement.

5.4.2.1 The Structure of the Celebration

The celebration typically spans an entire weekend, featuring a variety of activities designed to engage the community and promote awareness. These include:

- **Parades and Marches:** The festivities kick off with a vibrant parade through the heart of Tarvel, where participants don colorful attire, wave flags, and chant slogans that echo Adin's fight for freedom. This public display of solidarity reminds the community of the struggles faced and the victories won.

- **Workshops and Panels:** Throughout the weekend, educational workshops and panel discussions are held, focusing on topics such as mental health, intersectionality, and the importance of allyship. These sessions aim to empower individuals with knowledge and tools to continue Adin's work in their own lives.

- **Art Exhibitions:** Local artists are invited to showcase their work, celebrating LGBTQ+ identities and experiences. These exhibitions often include pieces that reflect Adin's journey and the broader narrative of LGBTQ+ rights.

- **Awards Ceremony:** A highlight of the celebration is the annual awards ceremony, where individuals and organizations that have made significant contributions to the LGBTQ+ community are recognized. This not only honors their efforts but also inspires others to engage in activism.

5.4.2.2 Theoretical Framework of Celebration

The act of celebrating achievements, especially in the context of social movements, can be understood through several theoretical lenses. One relevant framework is *Ritual Theory*, which posits that rituals serve to reinforce community bonds and collective identity. In the case of Adin's celebration, the rituals of parades, workshops, and awards serve to:

$$C = \sum_{i=1}^{n} R_i \tag{73}$$

where C represents community cohesion, and R_i represents the individual rituals performed during the celebration.

Moreover, the celebration can be viewed through the lens of *Collective Memory Theory*, which emphasizes the importance of shared experiences in shaping a group's identity. By commemorating Adin's achievements annually, the community not only honors the past but also creates a narrative that influences future generations.

5.4.2.3 Addressing Challenges

Despite the joyous nature of the celebration, there are challenges that arise each year. These include:

- **Opposition from Conservative Groups:** Each year, the celebration faces potential backlash from conservative factions within and outside Tarvel. This opposition often manifests in counter-protests or attempts to undermine the event's legitimacy. Organizers have learned to navigate these challenges by emphasizing dialogue and community outreach, fostering understanding rather than division.

- **Inclusivity:** Ensuring that the celebration is inclusive of all identities within the LGBTQ+ spectrum can be complex. Organizers strive to create an environment that acknowledges and respects the diverse experiences of community members, which requires ongoing education and sensitivity training for volunteers and participants.

- **Resource Allocation:** Funding and resources are perennial concerns for community organizers. Securing sponsorships and donations is crucial to ensuring the celebration can be executed at the desired scale. This necessitates strategic planning and outreach to potential allies and sponsors.

5.4.2.4 Examples of Impact

The impact of the annual celebration extends beyond the immediate festivities. For instance, the event has successfully raised significant funds for local LGBTQ+ organizations, enabling them to provide essential services such as mental health support and legal advocacy.

In one notable year, the celebration raised over $50,000, which was allocated to a local LGBTQ+ youth center, allowing them to expand their programs and reach more young people in need. This financial support is crucial in sustaining the momentum of Adin's legacy and ensuring that the community continues to thrive.

Additionally, the celebration has fostered a sense of pride and belonging among attendees. Many participants report feeling empowered and inspired to engage in activism after attending the event. Testimonials collected from attendees highlight how the celebration serves as a catalyst for individuals to take action in their own lives, whether through volunteering, advocacy, or simply being more open about their identities.

5.4.2.5 Conclusion

In conclusion, the annual celebration of Adin Xeris' achievements is more than just a commemoration; it is a vital part of the ongoing struggle for LGBTQ+ rights in Tarvel and beyond. By honoring Adin's legacy, the community not only reflects on past victories but also galvanizes support for future efforts. Through education, celebration, and collective action, the spirit of Adin Xeris lives on, inspiring new generations to continue the fight for equality and justice. As the community gathers each year, they are reminded that the journey is far from over, and together, they will strive for a world where love knows no bounds.

Epilogue

Epilogue

Epilogue

As we draw the curtain on the life and legacy of Adin Xeris, it is imperative to reflect on the revolutionary journey that not only transformed the landscape of LGBTQ+ rights in Tarvel but also resonated across the globe. Adin's journey was not merely a personal saga; it was a collective movement that challenged the status quo and ignited a spark of change in the hearts of many.

Lessons learned from Adin's activism

Adin's activism was rooted in the understanding that change is often born from the intersection of personal experience and collective struggle. One of the key lessons learned from Adin's activism is the importance of community. Adin often remarked, "Alone we can do so little; together we can do so much." This statement encapsulates the essence of grassroots movements, where each individual's story contributes to a larger narrative of resistance and resilience.

The theory of social movements posits that collective action can lead to significant societal change. According to Charles Tilly's framework, social movements operate through a series of processes that include mobilization, framing, and the establishment of political opportunities. Adin exemplified this by mobilizing local LGBTQ+ individuals, framing their struggles in a way that resonated with the broader community, and seizing political opportunities to advocate for legislative change.

The ongoing battle for LGBTQ+ rights worldwide

Despite the progress made in Tarvel, the battle for LGBTQ+ rights continues globally. Adin's legacy serves as a reminder that activism is an ongoing process, not a destination. The United Nations reports that in many parts of the world, LGBTQ+ individuals still face discrimination, violence, and systemic inequalities. The fight for equality is far from over, and it is crucial for new generations of activists to continue pushing for change.

For instance, in regions where LGBTQ+ rights are still heavily suppressed, activists often face severe repercussions for their efforts. The work of organizations like ILGA (International Lesbian, Gay, Bisexual, Trans and Intersex Association) highlights the need for global solidarity in the fight for human rights. Adin's commitment to international advocacy inspired many to look beyond local struggles and engage in a global dialogue about equality.

Tarvel's progress in LGBTQ+ equality after Adin

In the years following Adin's passing, Tarvel has witnessed significant strides in LGBTQ+ equality. The establishment of the Adin Xeris Memorial Foundation has played a pivotal role in promoting awareness and education about LGBTQ+ issues in schools and communities. Programs initiated by the foundation have focused on anti-bullying campaigns, inclusivity training, and mental health resources for LGBTQ+ youth.

Furthermore, Tarvel's local government has begun to implement policies that protect LGBTQ+ individuals from discrimination in housing, employment, and public services. This progress can be attributed to the groundwork laid by Adin and the activism of countless individuals who continue to fight for justice.

Global change inspired by Adin Xeris

Adin's influence has transcended borders, inspiring activists worldwide to adopt similar strategies in their own contexts. The concept of intersectionality, popularized by Kimberlé Crenshaw, emphasizes the interconnected nature of social categorizations such as race, class, and gender, which can create overlapping systems of discrimination. Adin's advocacy highlighted the importance of recognizing these intersections, thereby fostering a more inclusive movement.

For example, during the annual Pride Month celebrations, many activists now incorporate discussions around racial justice, economic inequality, and gender identity, reflecting the multifaceted nature of oppression. Adin's legacy encourages a holistic approach to activism that recognizes the diverse experiences within the LGBTQ+ community.

The next generation of LGBTQ+ activists

The torch of activism has been passed to a new generation, eager to continue the fight for equality. Young activists are utilizing social media platforms to amplify their voices, organize protests, and share personal stories that resonate with a global audience. The digital age has transformed activism, allowing for greater connectivity and solidarity among diverse groups.

Adin's story serves as a source of inspiration for these young activists, reminding them of the power of resilience and the importance of community. As they navigate the complexities of modern activism, they carry forward the lessons learned from Adin's journey, emphasizing collaboration, inclusivity, and the necessity of self-care in the face of adversity.

Adin's call to action and the importance of advocacy

Adin's life was a testament to the power of advocacy. Through tireless efforts, Adin demonstrated that every voice matters and that change is possible when individuals stand together. As we reflect on Adin's journey, we are reminded of the critical role each of us plays in the ongoing fight for LGBTQ+ rights.

The call to action is clear: we must remain vigilant, continue to educate ourselves and others, and advocate for those whose voices are marginalized. Whether through grassroots organizing, policy advocacy, or simply being an ally, each action contributes to a larger movement toward equality.

The ongoing work of Adin's memorial foundation

The Adin Xeris Memorial Foundation continues to honor Adin's legacy by supporting initiatives that promote education, awareness, and advocacy for LGBTQ+ rights. Through scholarships, community programs, and public awareness campaigns, the foundation ensures that Adin's vision for a more inclusive society lives on.

The foundation's annual events, such as the "Adin Xeris Day of Action," bring together individuals from all walks of life to celebrate diversity and promote LGBTQ+ rights. These gatherings not only serve as a tribute to Adin but also as a platform for continued activism and solidarity.

Annual celebrations of Adin's birthday and activism

Each year, on Adin's birthday, communities across Tarvel and beyond come together to celebrate Adin's life and the progress made in the fight for LGBTQ+ rights. These celebrations serve as a reminder of the ongoing struggle and the importance of unity in the face of adversity.

Through art, music, and storytelling, these events honor Adin's contributions while also highlighting the voices of those who continue to fight for equality. The legacy of Adin Xeris lives on in the hearts and minds of those who believe in the power of love, acceptance, and activism.

In conclusion, as we reflect on the revolutionary journey of Adin Xeris, we are reminded that the fight for LGBTQ+ rights is far from over. Adin's legacy serves as a beacon of hope, inspiring us to continue the work that lies ahead. The lessons learned from Adin's activism will guide us as we strive for a world where everyone, regardless of their sexual orientation or gender identity, can live freely and authentically.

Reflections on Adin Xeris' Revolutionary Journey

Lessons learned from Adin's activism

Adin Xeris' journey through the tumultuous landscape of LGBTQ activism in Tarvel offers invaluable lessons that resonate far beyond the borders of his hometown. His experiences illuminate the complexities of advocacy, the necessity of resilience, and the power of community in the relentless pursuit of equality. This subsection delves into the key lessons learned from Adin's activism, drawing on both theoretical frameworks and practical examples that highlight the significance of his contributions.

1. Understanding Intersectionality

One of the foremost lessons from Adin's activism is the critical importance of intersectionality in the fight for LGBTQ rights. Coined by legal scholar Kimberlé Crenshaw, intersectionality refers to the way various social identities—such as race, gender, sexual orientation, and class—interact to create unique modes of discrimination and privilege. Adin recognized early on that the LGBTQ community is not monolithic; it encompasses individuals with diverse backgrounds and experiences.

For instance, during the organization of the first LGBTQ Awareness March in Tarvel, Adin ensured that voices from marginalized groups within the LGBTQ spectrum were amplified.   This included collaborating with local Black and Indigenous activists who highlighted the specific challenges faced by queer people of color.   By fostering an inclusive dialogue, Adin was able to create a more comprehensive platform that addressed the needs of the entire community, rather than a select few.

2. The Power of Grassroots Movements

Adin's activism underscores the power of grassroots movements in effecting social change.   In a world where large organizations often dominate the narrative, Adin demonstrated that real change often starts at the community level.   His efforts to organize underground LGBTQ gatherings in Tarvel not only provided a safe space for individuals to express their identities but also laid the groundwork for a larger movement.

As Adin famously stated during one of his speeches, "Change doesn't come from the top; it bubbles up from the bottom." This philosophy guided his approach and led to the establishment of a local advocacy group that became instrumental in lobbying for anti-discrimination laws.   The success of these grassroots initiatives serves as a reminder that every voice matters, and collective action can lead to monumental shifts in societal attitudes.

3. Resilience in the Face of Adversity

Another vital lesson from Adin's journey is the necessity of resilience in the face of adversity.   Activism is fraught with challenges, and Adin encountered significant opposition from conservative groups throughout his career.   The backlash he faced during his early efforts to challenge Tarvel's marriage equality ban was intense, often manifesting in threats and public ridicule.

However, Adin's ability to remain steadfast in his convictions, even when the odds were stacked against him, is a testament to his character. He often turned to the community for support during these trying times, reinforcing the idea that resilience is not a solitary endeavor but rather a collective one. Adin's mantra, "Together, we are unbreakable," became a rallying cry for many, emphasizing the strength found in unity.

4. The Importance of Mental Health Awareness

Adin's activism also shed light on the often-overlooked intersection of mental health and activism. The pressures of advocating for LGBTQ rights can take a toll on mental well-being, as Adin experienced firsthand. His candid discussions about battling anxiety and depression resonated with many in the community, highlighting the importance of prioritizing mental health alongside activism.

By advocating for mental health resources within the LGBTQ community, Adin not only addressed his struggles but also encouraged others to seek help. He famously collaborated with mental health professionals to create workshops aimed at equipping activists with tools to manage stress and burnout. This initiative underscored the lesson that self-care is essential for sustaining long-term activism.

5. The Role of Education and Awareness

Lastly, Adin's activism emphasized the critical role of education and awareness in combating prejudice and discrimination. Through workshops, seminars, and public speaking engagements, he sought to educate both the LGBTQ community and the broader public about the issues at stake. Adin understood that knowledge is power, and by demystifying LGBTQ identities and experiences, he could foster empathy and understanding.

For example, during a particularly contentious town hall meeting, Adin utilized data from studies on LGBTQ youth mental health to advocate for inclusive policies in local schools. His ability to present facts in a relatable manner not only swayed opinions but also inspired others to engage in educational efforts within their own communities.

Conclusion

In conclusion, the lessons learned from Adin Xeris' activism serve as a powerful reminder of the complexities and nuances involved in the struggle for LGBTQ rights. By embracing intersectionality, harnessing the power of grassroots movements, demonstrating resilience, prioritizing mental health, and advocating for education, Adin forged a path that many continue to follow. His legacy is not just one of triumphs but also of the enduring lessons that empower future generations of activists to continue the fight for equality and justice.

The ongoing battle for LGBTQ+ rights worldwide

The struggle for LGBTQ+ rights is a relentless journey that transcends borders, cultures, and ideologies. While significant progress has been made in some regions, the global landscape remains fraught with challenges, discrimination, and violence against LGBTQ+ individuals. This section explores the ongoing battle for LGBTQ+ rights worldwide, examining the theoretical frameworks, persistent problems, and notable examples that highlight the urgency of this fight.

Theoretical Frameworks

To understand the ongoing battle for LGBTQ+ rights, it is essential to consider various theoretical frameworks that inform activism and policy-making. Among these, the **Intersectionality Theory**, coined by Kimberlé Crenshaw, is particularly relevant. Intersectionality posits that individuals experience oppression in varying degrees based on their intersecting identities, such as race, gender, class, and sexual orientation. This theory underscores the necessity for LGBTQ+ activism to address not only sexual orientation but also the myriad of factors that contribute to an individual's experience of discrimination.

Another critical framework is the **Social Justice Theory**, which advocates for equitable treatment and the dismantling of systems that perpetuate inequality. This perspective encourages activists to challenge not only discriminatory laws but also societal norms that foster prejudice and exclusion. By applying these theoretical lenses, activists can create more inclusive movements that resonate with diverse communities.

Persistent Problems

Despite advancements in some areas, numerous challenges hinder the progress of LGBTQ+ rights globally. These include:

- **Legal Discrimination:** In many countries, same-sex relationships remain criminalized, and LGBTQ+ individuals face legal barriers to marriage, adoption, and employment. According to a 2021 report by the International Lesbian, Gay, Bisexual, Trans and Intersex Association (ILGA), 69 countries still criminalize same-sex relationships, with penalties ranging from fines to imprisonment and even the death penalty in some regions.

- **Violence and Hate Crimes:** LGBTQ+ individuals are disproportionately affected by violence and hate crimes. The 2020 FBI Hate Crime Statistics report indicated that hate crimes based on sexual orientation accounted for approximately 16.7% of all hate crimes reported in the United States. Globally, trans individuals, particularly trans women of color, face alarming rates of violence, as highlighted by the Trans Murder Monitoring project, which reported over 350 murders of trans and gender-diverse individuals in 2020 alone.

- **Social Stigma and Discrimination:** Societal attitudes towards LGBTQ+ individuals often perpetuate discrimination and stigma. A 2021 survey by the Pew Research Center found that in many countries, a significant portion of the population still holds negative views towards LGBTQ+ individuals, which can lead to social ostracism and mental health challenges.

+ **Access to Healthcare:** LGBTQ+ individuals frequently encounter barriers to accessing healthcare, including discrimination from healthcare providers, lack of culturally competent care, and inadequate mental health services. The World Health Organization (WHO) emphasizes the need for inclusive healthcare policies to address these disparities.

Notable Examples of Ongoing Struggles

The ongoing battle for LGBTQ+ rights can be illustrated through various global examples:

+ **The United States:** The repeal of the "Don't Ask, Don't Tell" policy in 2011 marked a significant victory for LGBTQ+ rights in the military. However, the recent rise in anti-LGBTQ+ legislation, particularly targeting transgender individuals in sports and healthcare, underscores the fragility of these gains. Activists continue to mobilize against bills that seek to undermine the rights of LGBTQ+ individuals, emphasizing the need for vigilance and advocacy.

+ **Russia:** The 2013 "gay propaganda" law has resulted in widespread discrimination and violence against LGBTQ+ individuals. Activists face severe repression, and many have fled the country to seek asylum. The international community has condemned these actions, yet change remains elusive as the government continues to suppress LGBTQ+ rights under the guise of protecting traditional values.

+ **Africa:** In several African nations, LGBTQ+ individuals face harsh penalties, including imprisonment and violence. The situation in Uganda, where a proposed "Kill the Gays" bill garnered international outrage, exemplifies the extreme measures taken against LGBTQ+ individuals. Activists within and outside these regions work tirelessly to provide support and advocate for change, often at great personal risk.

+ **Asia:** Countries like India have made strides in LGBTQ+ rights, such as the decriminalization of homosexuality in 2018. However, societal stigma persists, and activists continue to fight for comprehensive anti-discrimination laws and societal acceptance. In contrast, countries like Indonesia have seen a rise in anti-LGBTQ+ sentiment, with public shaming and violence becoming more prevalent.

Call to Action

The ongoing battle for LGBTQ+ rights worldwide requires a unified effort from individuals, organizations, and governments. Activists must continue to raise awareness about the issues faced by LGBTQ+ individuals and work towards creating inclusive policies that protect their rights. This includes:

- **Advocating for Legal Reforms:** Lobbying for the repeal of discriminatory laws and the enactment of protective legislation is crucial. International organizations and local activists must collaborate to create pressure on governments to uphold human rights for all individuals, regardless of sexual orientation or gender identity.

- **Building Alliances:** Forming coalitions with other marginalized groups can amplify the voices of LGBTQ+ individuals. By addressing the interconnectedness of various social justice issues, activists can create a more comprehensive approach to advocacy.

- **Promoting Education and Awareness:** Education plays a vital role in changing societal attitudes. Initiatives that promote understanding and acceptance of LGBTQ+ individuals can help reduce stigma and discrimination.

- **Supporting Mental Health Initiatives:** Ensuring access to mental health resources for LGBTQ+ individuals is essential. Activists must advocate for inclusive healthcare policies that address the unique challenges faced by this community.

In conclusion, the ongoing battle for LGBTQ+ rights worldwide is a complex and multifaceted issue that requires persistent effort, strategic advocacy, and solidarity across borders. By understanding the theoretical frameworks, recognizing the persistent problems, and learning from notable examples, activists can continue to push for progress and equality for all LGBTQ+ individuals. The legacy of Adin Xeris serves as a reminder that the fight for LGBTQ+ rights is far from over, and the call to action remains urgent and essential.

Adin's Lasting Impact on Tarvel and the World

Tarvel's progress in LGBTQ+ equality after Adin

In the wake of Adin Xeris' monumental activism, Tarvel experienced a transformative shift in its approach to LGBTQ+ equality. The grassroots movements ignited by Adin laid the foundation for a more inclusive society, leading to significant legislative changes and a cultural reawakening. This section explores the progress made in Tarvel regarding LGBTQ+ rights, highlighting key developments and ongoing challenges.

Legislative Changes

Following the landmark Supreme Court case championed by Adin, which ruled against Tarvel's marriage equality ban, local lawmakers were pressured to reconsider existing discriminatory laws. The case, referred to as *Xeris v. Tarvel State*, served as a catalyst for change, illustrating the need for comprehensive anti-discrimination legislation. The ruling set a legal precedent, and in the subsequent years, Tarvel saw the introduction of several key policies:

+ **Anti-Discrimination Ordinances:** In 2022, the Tarvel City Council passed an ordinance prohibiting discrimination based on sexual orientation and gender identity in employment, housing, and public accommodations. This was a significant step forward, ensuring that LGBTQ+ individuals could live and work without fear of prejudice.

+ **Marriage Equality Implementation:** Following the Supreme Court's decision, marriage licenses were made available to same-sex couples, leading to a surge in LGBTQ+ weddings. Local businesses began to cater to this demographic, fostering a sense of community and acceptance.

+ **Transgender Rights Legislation:** In 2023, Tarvel implemented policies allowing individuals to change their gender markers on identification documents without requiring surgery. This legislative change was crucial for the transgender community, affirming their identities and rights.

Cultural Shifts

The activism spearheaded by Adin created a ripple effect that transcended legal changes. Cultural attitudes towards LGBTQ+ individuals began to evolve, with increased visibility and representation in various sectors:

- **Education Initiatives:** Local schools introduced LGBTQ+ history and awareness programs, aiming to educate students about diversity and inclusion. This curriculum shift was essential in combating homophobia and transphobia among younger generations.

- **Community Events:** The annual Tarvel Pride Parade, which began as a small gathering, grew into a city-wide celebration attracting thousands. This event not only promoted visibility but also served as a platform for LGBTQ+ voices to be heard.

- **Media Representation:** With the rise of LGBTQ+ narratives in local media, representation improved significantly. Local filmmakers and artists began to tell stories that reflected the experiences of LGBTQ+ individuals, fostering empathy and understanding within the broader community.

Challenges Ahead

Despite the progress made, Tarvel still faced challenges in its journey towards full equality. Issues such as discrimination in healthcare, mental health resources, and violence against LGBTQ+ individuals persisted. For instance, a 2024 survey indicated that 30% of LGBTQ+ individuals in Tarvel reported experiencing discrimination in healthcare settings. This statistic highlights the need for ongoing advocacy and education within the medical community.

Moreover, the rise of conservative backlash against LGBTQ+ rights posed a significant threat to the progress achieved. Groups opposing the advancements sought to roll back protections, leading to heated debates in local government meetings. Activists, inspired by Adin's legacy, continued to organize and advocate for the rights of marginalized communities, emphasizing the importance of solidarity and resilience.

Conclusion

Tarvel's progress in LGBTQ+ equality post-Adin Xeris is a testament to the power of activism and community engagement. While significant strides have been made, the journey is far from over. The foundation laid by Adin and the subsequent movements must be built upon, ensuring that future generations of LGBTQ+ individuals can live freely and authentically. As Tarvel continues to evolve, the spirit of Adin Xeris remains a guiding force, inspiring ongoing efforts towards justice and equality for all.

$$\text{Equality Progress} = \text{Legislative Change} + \text{Cultural Shift} - \text{Ongoing Challenges} \tag{74}$$

Global change inspired by Adin Xeris

Adin Xeris emerged as not just a local figurehead in Tarvel but as a beacon of hope and change on a global scale. His activism catalyzed movements far beyond the confines of his hometown, igniting a fire that spread across continents. This section delves into the profound global changes inspired by Adin Xeris, highlighting the theoretical frameworks, issues, and tangible outcomes that emerged as a result of his relentless fight for LGBTQ+ rights.

Theoretical Frameworks of Activism

Adin's activism can be analyzed through various theoretical lenses, including Social Movement Theory, which posits that collective action leads to social change. According to Tilly and Tarrow (2015), social movements are characterized by a combination of shared grievances, mobilization, and the ability to create a political opportunity structure. Adin's ability to articulate the struggles of the LGBTQ+ community in Tarvel resonated with similar movements worldwide, creating a ripple effect that galvanized activists in other regions.

Furthermore, the concept of Intersectionality, coined by Kimberlé Crenshaw (1989), emphasizes the interconnected nature of social categorizations such as race, class, and gender. Adin's advocacy was inclusive, addressing not only sexual orientation but also the broader spectrum of identities, thus encouraging activists globally to adopt a more holistic approach to their struggles.

Global Problems Addressed by Adin's Activism

Adin's journey highlighted several pressing global issues faced by the LGBTQ+ community, including:

+ **Discrimination and Violence:** Many countries still impose harsh penalties for LGBTQ+ identities. Adin's visibility and courage inspired campaigns against such laws, leading to a global outcry for justice.

+ **Mental Health Challenges:** The stigma surrounding LGBTQ+ individuals often results in high rates of mental health issues. By openly discussing his own struggles, Adin encouraged a global dialogue about mental health resources and support systems for queer individuals.

+ **Legal Inequality:** Adin's fight for legal rights in Tarvel served as a case study for activists in nations where marriage equality and anti-discrimination laws were still lacking. His advocacy underscored the necessity of legal frameworks that protect LGBTQ+ rights worldwide.

Examples of Global Change Inspired by Adin Xeris

Adin's influence can be seen in various global movements and initiatives:

1. **International Pride Events:** Following the success of LGBTQ+ events in Tarvel, cities around the world began organizing their own Pride marches, often drawing inspiration from Adin's grassroots organizing strategies. For instance, the annual Pride Parade in São Paulo, Brazil, has grown to be one of the largest in the world, celebrating diversity and inclusion.

2. **Formation of Global Advocacy Networks:** Adin's establishment of an advocacy group in Tarvel encouraged the formation of similar organizations globally. The network, now known as the Global LGBTQ+ Alliance, connects activists from various countries, providing resources and support for local initiatives.

3. **Policy Changes:** Adin's lobbying efforts in Tarvel set a precedent that inspired activists in countries like Kenya and Uganda, where LGBTQ+ rights are severely restricted. Following his model, activists successfully campaigned for the repeal of discriminatory laws in several regions, leading to significant policy changes.

Measuring Impact: A Quantitative Approach

The impact of Adin's activism can also be measured through quantitative data. For instance, a survey conducted by the International LGBTQ+ Rights Coalition (ILRC) in 2022 revealed that:

$$\text{Increase in LGBTQ+ Rights Awareness} = \frac{\text{Number of Countries with New LGBTQ+ Pr}}{\text{Total Number of Countries}}$$
$$(75)$$

This formula demonstrated a 25% increase in the number of countries adopting new legal protections for LGBTQ+ individuals since Adin's rise as an activist.

Furthermore, the increase in mental health resources available to LGBTQ+ individuals can be represented by:

$$\text{Mental Health Resource Growth} = \frac{\text{New LGBTQ+ Focused Mental Health Programs}}{\text{Total Mental Health Programs}} \times 1$$

$$\tag{76}$$

This showed a growth of 40% in programs specifically designed to address the unique challenges faced by LGBTQ+ individuals in the past five years.

Conclusion

In conclusion, Adin Xeris's activism transcended borders, influencing a global movement for LGBTQ+ rights. Through theoretical frameworks of social movements and intersectionality, the problems he addressed resonated with activists worldwide. The tangible examples of global change, supported by quantitative data, illustrate the lasting legacy of Adin's work. His journey serves as a reminder that the fight for equality is a collective endeavor, one that continues to inspire new generations to challenge injustice and advocate for a more inclusive world.

Continuing the Fight

The next generation of LGBTQ+ activists

The legacy of Adin Xeris serves as a catalyst for the next generation of LGBTQ+ activists, who are now stepping into the spotlight with a unique blend of passion, creativity, and technological savvy. This new wave of activists understands that the landscape of advocacy has evolved, and they are armed with tools that previous generations could only dream of.

Theoretical Framework

To contextualize the emergence of these activists, we can draw upon the *Social Movement Theory*, which posits that social movements arise in response to perceived injustices and that they are driven by collective identity and mobilization. The next generation is navigating a complex intersection of identities, including race, gender, and sexuality, which adds layers to their activism.

The *Intersectionality Theory*, coined by Kimberlé Crenshaw, emphasizes how different social categorizations overlap and create unique experiences of discrimination and privilege. This framework is crucial for understanding how younger activists are not just fighting for LGBTQ+ rights, but are also addressing issues like racial justice, economic inequality, and climate change within their activism.'

Challenges Faced

Despite the advantages they have, the next generation of LGBTQ+ activists faces significant challenges. One major issue is the *backlash* against progressive movements. For instance, in many regions, anti-LGBTQ+ legislation has surged, with lawmakers targeting the rights of transgender individuals, particularly in sports and healthcare. This backlash creates a hostile environment that can dissuade young activists from fully engaging in advocacy.

Moreover, there is the challenge of *digital activism fatigue*. While social media platforms provide a space for activism and community building, they can also lead to burnout. Activists often find themselves inundated with negative comments, harassment, and the overwhelming nature of online discourse. The pressure to maintain a constant online presence can detract from their mental health and the effectiveness of their advocacy.

Examples of Activism

Nonetheless, the next generation is not backing down. Organizations like *Generation Equality* and *The Trevor Project* are led by young activists who are redefining what it means to advocate for LGBTQ+ rights. For example, the *March for Our Lives* movement, initially focused on gun control, has expanded to include LGBTQ+ issues, with young leaders using their platform to highlight the intersections of violence against marginalized communities.

In addition, grassroots movements like *Trans Lifeline* and *Black Trans Advocacy Coalition* exemplify how the next generation is prioritizing the voices of the most marginalized within the LGBTQ+ community. These organizations are often led by individuals who have lived experiences that inform their activism, ensuring that their work is both relevant and impactful.

The Role of Technology

Technology plays a pivotal role in shaping the activism of this new generation. Platforms such as TikTok and Instagram allow activists to share their messages in innovative ways, using humor, art, and storytelling to engage a broader audience. For instance, viral campaigns like *#BlackLivesMatter* have successfully integrated

LGBTQ+ issues, showcasing the interconnectedness of various social justice movements.

The use of data analytics in campaigns has also become more prevalent. Activists are now able to track engagement, understand demographic shifts, and tailor their messages accordingly. This data-driven approach allows for more strategic advocacy, making it easier to mobilize supporters and generate impactful change.

Conclusion

In conclusion, the next generation of LGBTQ+ activists is poised to continue the work of pioneers like Adin Xeris, but they do so with a fresh perspective and new tools at their disposal. By embracing the complexities of intersectionality and leveraging technology, they are not only addressing the challenges of today but are also laying the groundwork for a more inclusive and equitable future. As they carry forward the torch of activism, it is essential for allies and older generations to support and uplift these young voices, ensuring that the fight for LGBTQ+ rights remains vibrant and resilient.

$$\text{Activism}_{\text{next gen}} = \text{Intersectionality} + \text{Technology} + \text{Community Support} - \text{Fatigue} \tag{77}$$

Adin's call to action and the importance of advocacy

Adin Xeris, a name that became synonymous with the fight for LGBTQ+ rights in Tarvel, understood that advocacy was not merely a role to be played but a lifelong commitment to justice and equality. His journey illuminated the importance of advocacy, not just for the LGBTQ+ community, but for all marginalized groups.

Theoretical Framework of Advocacy

Advocacy can be framed through several theoretical lenses, including the Social Change Theory and the Empowerment Theory. The Social Change Theory posits that effective advocacy leads to significant societal transformations. This is evident in how Adin's activism influenced local legislation and shifted public perception regarding LGBTQ+ rights.

$$\text{Social Change} = f(\text{Advocacy Efforts, Community Engagement}) \tag{78}$$

Where f represents the function of advocacy efforts and community engagement in driving social change. Adin's tireless work exemplified this theory, as he mobilized community members to engage in activism, thereby amplifying their voices.

Identifying Problems and Barriers

Despite the progress made, Adin recognized that numerous barriers hindered the advancement of LGBTQ+ rights. These included:

+ **Institutional Discrimination:** Laws and policies that perpetuated inequality, such as marriage bans and anti-discrimination legislation.

+ **Social Stigma:** Deep-rooted prejudices that marginalized LGBTQ+ individuals, leading to mental health issues and societal exclusion.

+ **Lack of Representation:** Insufficient visibility of LGBTQ+ individuals in media and politics, which perpetuated stereotypes and misinformation.

Adin's advocacy addressed these barriers head-on, emphasizing the need for systemic change and societal acceptance.

Call to Action

Adin's call to action was clear: every individual has a role to play in the advocacy landscape. He believed that advocacy should be inclusive, encouraging participation from all sectors of society. His mantra, "If you see something, say something," resonated deeply, urging individuals to speak out against injustice, whether it was in their communities, workplaces, or online platforms.

$$\text{Advocacy Participation} = \text{Awareness} + \text{Action} \qquad (79)$$

This equation illustrates that awareness alone is insufficient; it must be coupled with action to effect change. Adin's life was a testament to this belief, as he demonstrated how individuals could mobilize for a cause, regardless of their background.

Real-World Examples

Adin's advocacy efforts were not without challenges, yet they yielded tangible results. For instance, during the first LGBTQ+ Awareness March in Tarvel, Adin rallied hundreds of supporters, showcasing the power of collective action. This event not only raised awareness but also garnered media attention, forcing local politicians to address LGBTQ+ rights publicly.

Additionally, Adin's formation of an advocacy group created a structured approach to fighting for legal rights. By organizing workshops, training sessions, and community outreach programs, he empowered individuals to become advocates themselves.

$$\text{Empowerment} = \text{Knowledge} + \text{Resources} \tag{80}$$

This equation highlights how Adin's initiatives provided community members with the knowledge and resources necessary to advocate effectively for their rights.

Legacy of Advocacy

Adin's legacy is a reminder that advocacy is an ongoing journey. He inspired a new generation of activists, encouraging them to continue the fight for equality. The importance of advocacy lies not only in achieving immediate goals but also in fostering a culture of activism that can sustain itself over time.

$$\text{Legacy of Advocacy} = \text{Impact} \times \text{Sustainability} \tag{81}$$

Where Impact refers to the changes achieved through advocacy, and Sustainability denotes the ability of movements to continue beyond the initial efforts.

In conclusion, Adin Xeris's call to action serves as a rallying cry for everyone to engage in advocacy. The importance of advocacy cannot be overstated; it is the lifeblood of social movements and the key to achieving lasting change. As we reflect on Adin's journey, let us remember that the fight for justice is a collective responsibility, one that requires courage, commitment, and an unwavering belief in the power of community.

The Legacy of Adin Xeris Lives On

The ongoing work of Adin's memorial foundation

Adin Xeris' memorial foundation, established shortly after their passing, has become a beacon of hope and resilience for the LGBTQ+ community in Tarvel and beyond. The foundation's mission is to honor Adin's legacy by continuing the fight for equality, providing support for LGBTQ+ youth, and advocating for mental health awareness. This section will delve into the ongoing work of the foundation, highlighting its initiatives, challenges, and impact.

1.1 Foundation Initiatives

The foundation has launched several key initiatives aimed at fostering inclusivity and support within the community. These initiatives include:

- **Scholarship Programs:** The foundation offers scholarships for LGBTQ+ youth pursuing higher education. This program not only alleviates financial burdens but also empowers young individuals to pursue their dreams in an accepting environment. The scholarship application process emphasizes personal stories of resilience, echoing Adin's own journey.

- **Mental Health Workshops:** Recognizing the mental health challenges faced by LGBTQ+ individuals, the foundation hosts workshops that focus on coping strategies, resilience, and self-acceptance. These workshops are led by licensed therapists who specialize in LGBTQ+ issues, providing a safe space for participants to share their experiences.

- **Advocacy Campaigns:** The foundation actively participates in advocacy campaigns aimed at influencing local legislation. By collaborating with other LGBTQ+ organizations, the foundation amplifies its voice, pushing for policies that protect against discrimination and promote equality. This includes lobbying for comprehensive anti-discrimination laws and marriage equality.

- **Community Outreach Programs:** The foundation conducts outreach programs in schools to educate students about LGBTQ+ issues, aiming to foster understanding and acceptance from a young age. These programs utilize interactive workshops and guest speakers, including prominent LGBTQ+ activists, to engage students in meaningful discussions.

1.2 Challenges Faced by the Foundation

Despite its noble mission, the foundation encounters several challenges in its ongoing work. Some of the most pressing issues include:

- **Funding Constraints:** Securing consistent funding is a significant challenge for the foundation. While initial donations poured in following Adin's passing, sustaining financial support has proven difficult. The foundation relies heavily on fundraising events and grants, which can be unpredictable. This instability limits the scope of its initiatives and outreach efforts.

+ **Resistance from Conservative Groups:** The foundation often faces backlash from conservative groups that oppose its advocacy efforts. This resistance can manifest in protests at events or public campaigns aimed at discrediting the foundation's work. Such opposition can create a hostile environment for both the foundation and the LGBTQ+ community it serves.

+ **Mental Health Stigma:** Despite increasing awareness, mental health stigma remains prevalent, particularly within conservative circles. This stigma can deter individuals from seeking help or participating in the foundation's mental health programs. The foundation continually works to combat this stigma through education and open dialogues.

1.3 Impact of the Foundation's Work

The impact of Adin's memorial foundation has been profound, shaping the landscape of LGBTQ+ advocacy in Tarvel. Some notable outcomes include:

+ **Increased Awareness:** Through its outreach programs and advocacy campaigns, the foundation has significantly raised awareness about LGBTQ+ issues in Tarvel. Schools that previously lacked LGBTQ+ education now incorporate discussions about acceptance and diversity into their curricula, fostering a more inclusive environment for all students.

+ **Empowerment of LGBTQ+ Youth:** The scholarship program has empowered numerous LGBTQ+ youth to pursue higher education, helping them break the cycle of poverty and discrimination. Many scholarship recipients have gone on to become advocates themselves, continuing Adin's legacy of activism.

+ **Strengthened Community Ties:** The foundation has created a network of support within the LGBTQ+ community, connecting individuals who might otherwise feel isolated. This sense of belonging is crucial for mental health and overall well-being, providing a safe haven for those navigating their identities.

1.4 Conclusion

The ongoing work of Adin's memorial foundation exemplifies the power of community and resilience in the face of adversity. By continuing Adin's mission, the foundation not only honors their legacy but also inspires a new generation of activists. As it navigates the challenges ahead, the foundation remains committed to fostering equality, acceptance, and mental health awareness, ensuring that Adin's spirit lives on in the hearts of many.

In the words of Adin, "Our fight is not just for ourselves; it's for the generations to come. We must pave the way for a world where love knows no bounds." This guiding principle continues to motivate the foundation's efforts, reminding us that the battle for equality is ongoing, and every voice matters in this crucial fight.

Annual celebrations of Adin's birthday and activism

Every year, on the anniversary of Adin Xeris' birth, the community of Tarvel and LGBTQ+ activists around the globe come together to celebrate not only the life of a revolutionary figure but also the ongoing fight for equality and acceptance. These celebrations serve as a poignant reminder of the struggles faced by the LGBTQ+ community and the strides made towards securing their rights.

The Significance of the Celebration

Adin's birthday has transformed into a day of reflection and action. It is a time to honor Adin's legacy, which is deeply rooted in the principles of love, acceptance, and relentless activism. The celebrations highlight the importance of community solidarity and serve as a platform for raising awareness about current LGBTQ+ issues.

Themes and Activities

Each year, the celebration centers around specific themes that resonate with the ongoing struggles of the LGBTQ+ community. For example, the theme for the 2023 celebration was *"Unity in Diversity,"* emphasizing the need for inclusivity within the LGBTQ+ spectrum. Activities during the celebrations include:

+ **Parades and Marches:** Colorful parades fill the streets of Tarvel, echoing the spirit of the first LGBTQ Awareness March organized by Adin. Participants don vibrant clothing, wave flags, and chant slogans that encapsulate the fight for equality.

+ **Workshops and Panels:** Educational workshops are held to discuss various topics, such as mental health in the LGBTQ+ community, the importance of allyship, and the history of LGBTQ+ rights. Panels featuring prominent activists and community leaders provide insights into the current landscape of LGBTQ+ activism.

+ **Art Exhibitions:** Local artists showcase their work, reflecting the themes of love, identity, and resistance. These exhibitions serve as a reminder of the power of art in activism and the importance of representation.

+ **Fundraising Events:** Fundraisers are organized to support local LGBTQ+ organizations and initiatives. The funds raised are often directed towards scholarships for LGBTQ+ youth, mental health resources, and community support services.

Community Involvement

The annual celebrations foster a sense of community and encourage participation from individuals of all backgrounds. Local businesses often contribute by sponsoring events or offering discounts to participants. Schools and universities engage students in discussions and activities, promoting awareness and education about LGBTQ+ issues.

Reflection and Remembrance

The celebrations also include moments of reflection, where community members share personal stories about how Adin's activism impacted their lives. These narratives serve as powerful testaments to the transformative effect of advocacy and the importance of visibility in the fight for rights.

$$\text{Impact} = \text{Advocacy} + \text{Visibility} + \text{Community Support} \tag{82}$$

This equation illustrates the essential components required to create meaningful change within the LGBTQ+ community. The impact of Adin's legacy continues to resonate, inspiring new generations of activists to carry the torch forward.

Conclusion

The annual celebrations of Adin Xeris' birthday are not merely commemorative events; they are vital expressions of resilience, hope, and the ongoing quest for justice. Each year, as the community gathers to celebrate, they reaffirm their commitment to the ideals that Adin championed. Through joy, remembrance, and action, they ensure that Adin's spirit lives on, guiding the fight for LGBTQ+ rights and equality in Tarvel and beyond.

As we look to the future, it is crucial to remember that the legacy of Adin Xeris is not just about the past but also about the ongoing journey towards a more inclusive and equitable world for all.

Index